MODALOGY

scales, modes & chords: the primordial building blocks of music

by Jeff Brent with Schell Barkley

ISBN 978-1-4584-1397-0

HAL•LEONARD®
CORPORATION

7777 W. BLUEMOUND RD. P.O. BOX 13819 MILWAUKEE, WI 53213

In Australia Contact:
Hal Leonard Australia Pty. Ltd.
4 Lentara Court
Cheltenham, Victoria, 3192 Australia
Email: ausadmin@halleonard.com.au

Visit Hal Leonard Online at
www.halleonard.com

Foreword

This is a book for musicians who are passionate about their craft—so passionate that they want to know where it comes from, how it works, and what its possibilities are. This volume is not a casual read, but if you want to thoroughly understand the melodic and harmonic function of scales and modes, Brent and Barkley will take you on a fascinating journey.

Modalogy begins, well, at the very beginning, with a look at some basic laws of physics involving intervals and the overtone series. Through a step-by-step process, the authors go on to trace the evolution of the pentatonic scale, major scale, modes, and ultimately all of the scales commonly employed by jazz musicians.

Throughout the discussion, they make it clear that all scales (yes, even symmetrical scales—and there are more than you think!) are formed as logical extensions of the basic major scale modes, which themselves are simply collections of consonant fourths derived from the overtone series.

The advantage to examining a scale in terms of its derivation and component parts is that you gain a basic understanding of its inherent characteristics and why it behaves the way it does. The authors elaborate on this as they discuss the cadences and progressions of the various modes one-by-one. We may know from experience that bII-i cadences are effective in Phrygian modes, while bVII-i cadences work well in Aeolian modes, but few of us have explored the reasons why.

The section on The Chromatic Modes is challenging, but also fascinating and worth delving into. The only 'criticism' I could conjure up was, *"Well, I don't think of it that way, but I wonder what other possibilities these concepts might open up for me?"*

This book has been carefully thought out, and explores musical relationships that many of us never dreamed were possible. Few individuals, including musicians, take the time to discover or appreciate the innate mathematical beauty of how music is put together. *"Unified field theory"* is an appropriate subtitle for this volume. It's just uncanny how the surface complexity of music reduces to utter simplicity and sheer logic.

Although some will read the volume cover-to-cover (not at one sitting!), others will find it more suited as a reference work. The copious appendices cover a broad array of topics with clear tables and charts.

If your approach to music theory is, *"I know what works, but I want to know why and what else I might explore,"* then this is the book for you.

Dr. Robert Rawlins
Coordinator of Music Theory and Chair of the Department of Music at Rowan University Author of *"Jazzology: The Encyclopedia of Jazz Theory for All Musicians"* (with N.E. Bahha) and *"A Simple and Direct Guide to Jazz Improvisation"* (Hal Leonard Corp).

Dec. 18, 2010

Table of Contents

The Relationship of the Fundamental to its Fifth and Fourth

Assuming a base frequency of the note "A" at 110Hz
(110 cycles per second)

The first overtone is 2X the original 110 cycles per second. Doubling the Hz results in the same note, but an octave higher, ie. "A" 220Hz.

The next is 3 times the original fundamental frequency. This results in 330Hz - "E" the fifth.

Then four times the fundamental equals "A" 440.

Due to "E" being an even multiple of an "A" (whichever "A" you care to choose - 110, 220, 440, 880, etc) these two notes are clearly consonant with each other.

Note that the relationship between "E" 330 and "A" 440 is the interval of a perfect fourth.

Intervals of both a fourth and a fifth (either above or below a given fundamental note) are completely consonant with that central note.

Examples:

"A" 220 is consonant with "E" 330 (a perfect fifth).

"E" 330 is also consonant with "A" 440 (a perfect fourth).

The origins of the minor pentatonic, the major scale, and the most common altered scales are the logical extensions of these basic laws of physics.

The Evolution of the Pentatonic Scale

Centered at D, the two most harmonically consonant notes with D
(as with any base note)
are both a perfect fourth above or a perfect fourth below

D

4th   4th

A   **D**   **G**

(figure 1)

D harmonizes perfectly with either A or G,
so why shouldn't the fourths surrounding THOSE two notes be consonant also?

Using the knowledge that 4ths harmonize either up or down, it is a simple matter to expand that formula to the interval of a perfect fourth on either side of figure 1:

4th   4th   4th   4th

E   **A**   **D**   **G**   **C**

(figure 2)

Rearranging the order of the radially symmetrical pitch set in figure 2,
one will notice that it is the Ur-Scale: "A minor pentatonic"

A   **C**   **D**   **E**   **G**

(figure 3)

Scales built with this same formula continue to have a lasting place in musics
all over the globe.

Root Tendencies in the Minor Pentatonic Scale

Establishing the tonic as A, the following tendency relationships exist within the roots in the minor pentatonic scale (A C D E G).

V-I (E-A) Alpha/Authentic Cadence
IV-I (D-A) Beta/Plagal Cadence
♭VII-I (G-A) Gamma Cadence

figure 4

All of the above root motions have a strong cadential pull to resolve to the A minor pentatonic's final tonic.

Note that these strong root motions which occur in the minor pentatonic ur-scale are echoed within the diatonic seven-note tonalities:

V-I Cadences

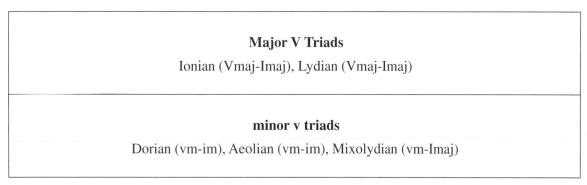

Major V Triads
Ionian (Vmaj-Imaj), Lydian (Vmaj-Imaj)
minor v triads
Dorian (vm-im), Aeolian (vm-im), Mixolydian (vm-Imaj)

figure 5

Major V triads provide a much stronger resolution to the tonic than do the weaker minor v motions due to the leading tone tendency inherent in the major third of the chord. As will be seen, each individual tonality has its own distinct set of rules.

IV-I Cadences

Major IV Triads
Ionian (IVmaj-Imaj), Mixolydian (IVmaj-Imaj), Dorian (IVmaj-im)
minor iv triads
Aeolian (ivm-im), Phrygian (ivm-im)

figure 6

♭VII-I Cadences

Major ♭VII Triads
Aeolian (♭VIImaj-im), Mixolydian (♭VII-Imaj), Dorian (♭VIImaj-im)
minor bvii triads
Phrygian (♭viim-im)

figure 7

Harmonizing the A Minor Pentatonic Roots with Perfect Fifths

The obvious first choice for a consonant interval to harmonize with a root are the fifths which exist within the A minor pentatonic scale.

A – E (1 – 5)
C – G (♭3 – V/♭3)
D – A (4 – V/4)
G – D (♭7 – V/♭7)

figure 8

The only note in the A minor pentatonic scale which does not possess a fifth is the V of the scale (E). Its harmony note is typically the ♭VII (G) which are the defining two notes of an E minor triad.

Adding fifths into the harmonic mix reinforces the cadential tendencies listed in figure 4. However, these strong root motion tendencies are dependent neither on the inclusion nor exclusion of a fifth (or for that matter a third).

The open IV chord D5 needs to resolve to the tonic A5 exactly as every plagal (beta) cadence does (Ionian, Dorian, etc).

Similarly, the open ♭VII chord G5 needs to resolve to the A5 tonic exactly as every gamma cadence does (Aeolian, Mixolydian, Dorian).

Harmonizing the A Minor Pentatonic Roots with Thirds

There are only three roots in the A minor pentatonic scale that possess thirds:

A's third is C (m3)
C's third is E (M3)
E's third is G (m3)
Both G and D lack thirds

figure 9

Both A and C are capable of generating full triads (A C E – the minor triad, and CEG - the major triad).

Note that the motion C5-A5 or C5-Am has a relatively strong tendency to resolve to the tonic A, yet when both chords include thirds in their structures this resolution tendency is weakened by the relationship between the common notes shared.

An Am-Cmaj or Cmaj-Am motion sounds more like a change of color as opposed to a strong root movement.

Root Tendencies in the Major Pentatonic Scale

While the major pentatonic scale cannot boast of possessing three cadences (as can the A minor pentatonic), the one it does have is the Authentic Alpha Cadence, the strongest of the lot:

$$G \rightarrow C$$
$$V \rightarrow I$$

In addition, it also possesses the ubiquitous II-V-I circular progression

$$D \rightarrow G \rightarrow C$$
$$II \rightarrow V \rightarrow I$$

to which each root's respective fifth can be added (which reinforces the strong chord motion tendencies to resolve up a fourth to arrive at the tonic):

$$D5 \rightarrow G5 \rightarrow C5$$
$$II \rightarrow V \rightarrow I$$

The A root also possesses a fifth and can be added to this chain of chords, which yields the familiar VI-II-V-I progression:

$$A5 \rightarrow D5 \rightarrow G5 \rightarrow C5$$
$$VI \rightarrow II \rightarrow V \rightarrow I$$

Constructing a two-note harmony by adding either 3rds, 5ths or 7ths to the roots, this example of a five chord circular chain is one possibility:

$$Em \rightarrow A7(open) \rightarrow D7(open) \rightarrow G5 \rightarrow Cmaj$$
$$iiim \rightarrow VI\ open \rightarrow II\ open \rightarrow V\ open \rightarrow I\ Major$$

Constructing three-note chords by adding 3rds, 5ths, 7ths and 9ths could yield the following pentatonic harmonies:

$$Em7 \rightarrow Am7 \rightarrow D9(open) \rightarrow G6(open) \rightarrow C6$$
$$iiim7 \rightarrow vim7 \rightarrow II7\ open \rightarrow V\ open \rightarrow I\ Major$$

Four-note harmony example (also see pg 215):

$$Em7sus4 \rightarrow Am7sus4 \rightarrow D9sus4 \rightarrow G69(open) \rightarrow C69$$
$$iiim7 \rightarrow vim7 \rightarrow II7sus4 \rightarrow V \rightarrow I\ Major$$

As can be seen from the previous page, the rock-solid principles and foundations of all harmony and harmonic root motion exist already in the pentatonics (2nd level of radially symmetrical consonance) - with or without the presence of the diatonic tritone (at the 3rd level of rs consonance).

These pentatonic harmonic principles include:

- Cadences (V-I, IV-I, ♭VII-I)
- Progressions (circular and modal)
- Basic Chord Qualities (minor triad, major triad, m7, 6th, suspensions)
- Harmonization by adding thirds, fifths, sevenths, ninths and 11ths
- Guide Tone Lines implicit between the inner chord motions

The addition of the tritone notes B and F to the pentatonic scale does not alter the functions already previously established in the realms of the minor and major pentatonics.

Adding the natural 7th (B) to any of the existing pentatonic chords does not change the function or quality of the chord as it is already manifested in the pentatonic realm (with one notable exception), but acts rather as either an enhancement, or color tone.

Examples:

- Add a B (♮7) to the C major triad, it's still a major quality chord.

- Add the B (♮6) to a D minor triad, it's still a minor quality chord.

- The B is the fifth of the E minor triad.

- Substitute the B (♭5) for the C(5) of an F major triad (or an Fmaj7) and it's still a major quality chord (with a non-functional tritone).

- B is the third of the G major triad. This is an enhancement, but its functional motion remains the same as in the major pentatonic (G resolves up a 4th to C).

- Adding a B to the Am7 which exists in the pentatonic, results in a minor 9th chord, which is still a minor quality chord.

- The 3rd level B creates a tritone with its counterpart the 3rd level F. This is an enhancement, which (in the major) reinforces the tendency of the V chord to resolve to the I chord (as previously established in the pentatonic).

The F is more problematic. It is a chord component in 4 cases (Dm, Fmaj, Bdim and G7) and clashes in three (Cmaj, Am, Em).

The addition of the F and the B creates

new triads
Dm, Em, Fmaj, Gmaj, Bdim

new chord qualities
dominant G7 and B half-diminished 7

new colors
maj7, maj7♭5, m9, m11, etc.

The Evolution of the Major Scale

Choosing D as our central note, the two most harmonically consonant notes are either a perfect fourth above or a perfect fourth below

D

4th   4th

A   **D**   **G**

(figure 10)

As seen, D harmonizes perfectly with either A or G.

Expanding that formula to the interval of a perfect fourth on either side of figure 10 yields the 2nd level of rs consonance:

4th   4th   4th   4th

E   **A**   **D**   **G**   **C**

(figure 11)

Rearranging the order of the notes in figure 2,
it is the Ur-Scale: "A minor pentatonic"

A   **C**   **D**   **E**   **G**

(figure 12)

Taking this "logic of 4ths" (as in page 2 figure 2) one step further,
the following 7-note pitch set was discovered (3rd level of rs consonance)

4th   4th   4th   4th   4th   4th

B   **E**   **A**   **D**   **G**   **C**   **F**

(figure 13)

which rearranged similarly to figure 12 above,
yields the radially symmetrical structure which is commonly known as
the "natural minor" or "Aeolian mode".

A   **B**   **C**   **D**   **E**   **F**   **G**

(figure 14)

This formula of scale degrees, continues to be in the top three favorite tonal centers for most musicians and composers.

The addition of the notes B and F into the A minor pentatonic scale, creates an interval of great tension, this special interval is known as a "tri-tone" (the interval of 3 whole-tones).

The tension created by the tritone calls for
the B to resolve up a half step to the C,
and for the F to resolve chromatically down to the E.

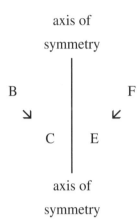

Once this radially symmetrical harmonic movement (cadence) has taken place, the natural resolution falls squarely on the two defining notes of the C major triad (C and E).

The introduction of the unstable tritone and its tendency to collapse symmetrically to resolve to the two defining components of the C major triad is the reason that the seven-note pitch set of the tonal center of "C major" became so popular.

These tension-resolution tendencies cement the major scale's dominance over all other scales.

C   D   E   F   G   A   B
(figure 15)

Ionian Set Modes Table

Ionian

I		II		III	IV		V		VI		VII	I

Dorian

I		II	♭III		IV		V		VI	♭VII		I

Phrygian

I	♭II		♭III		IV		V	♭VI		♭VII		I

Lydian

I		II		III		♯IV	V		VI		VII	I

Mixolydian

I		II		III	IV		V		VI	♭VII		I

Aeolian

I		II	♭III		IV		V	♭VI		♭VII		I

Locrian

I	♭II		♭III		IV	♭V		♭VI		♭VII		I

For modes of the jazz minor, harmonic minor and harmonic major, see pages 155–158.

Table of Ionian Set Modes

Ionian

I		II		III		IV		V		VI		VII		I
	1		1		½		1		1		1		½	

figure 16

Dorian (relative)

II		III		IV		V		VI		VII		I		II
	1		½		1		1		1		½		1	

figure 17

Dorian (parallel)

I		II		♭III		IV		V		VI		♭VII		I
	1		½		1		1		1		½		1	

figure 18

Phrygian (relative)

III		IV		V		VI		VII		I		II		III
	½		1		1		1		½		1		1	

figure 19

Phrygian (parallel)

I		♭II		♭III		IV		V		♭VI		♭VII		I
	½		1		1		1		½		1		1	

figure 20

Lydian (relative)

IV		V		VI		VII		I		II		III		IV
	1		1		1		½		1		1		½	

figure 21

Lydian (parallel)

I		II		III		♯IV		V		VI		VII		I
	1		1		1		½		1		1		½	

figure 22

Mixolydian (relative)

V		VI		VII		I		II		III		IV		V
	1		1		½		1		1		½		1	

figure 23

Mixolydian (parallel)

I		II		III		IV		V		VI		♭VII		I
	1		1		½		1		1		½		1	

figure 24

Aeolian (relative)

VI		VII		I		II		III		IV		V		VI
	1		½		1		1		½		1		1	

figure 25

Aeolian (parallel)

I		II		♭III		IV		V		♭VI		♭VII		I
	1		½		1		1		½		1		1	

figure 26

Locrian (relative)

VII		I		II		III		IV		V		VI		VII
	½		1		1		½		1		1		1	

figure 27

Locrian (parallel)

I		♭II		♭III		IV		♭V		♭VI		♭VII		I
	½		1		1		½		1		1		1	

figure 28

Ionian Sets Triads Table

I	ii	iii	IV	V	vi	vii°
C	Dm	Em	F	G	Am	B°
G	Am	Bm	C	D	Em	F♯°
D	Em	F♯m	G	A	Bm	C♯°
A	Bm	C♯m	D	E	F♯m	G♯°
E	F♯m	G♯m	A	B	C♯m	D♯°
B	C♯m	D♯m	E	F♯	G♯m	A♯°
C♭	D♭m	E♭m	F♭	G♭	A♭m	B♭°
F♯	G♯m	A♯m	B	C♯	D♯m	E♯°
G♭	A♭m	B♭m	C♭	D♭	E♭m	F°
C♯	D♯m	E♯m	F♯	G♯	A♯m	B♯°
D♭	E♭m	Fm	G♭	A♭	B♭m	C°
A♭	B♭m	Cm	D♭	E♭	Fm	G°
E♭	Fm	Gm	A♭	B♭	Cm	D°
B♭	Cm	Dm	E♭	F	Gm	A°
F	Gm	Am	B♭	C	Dm	E°
C	Dm	Em	F	G	Am	B°

The Relationship Between Ionian Set Triads

Major Scale

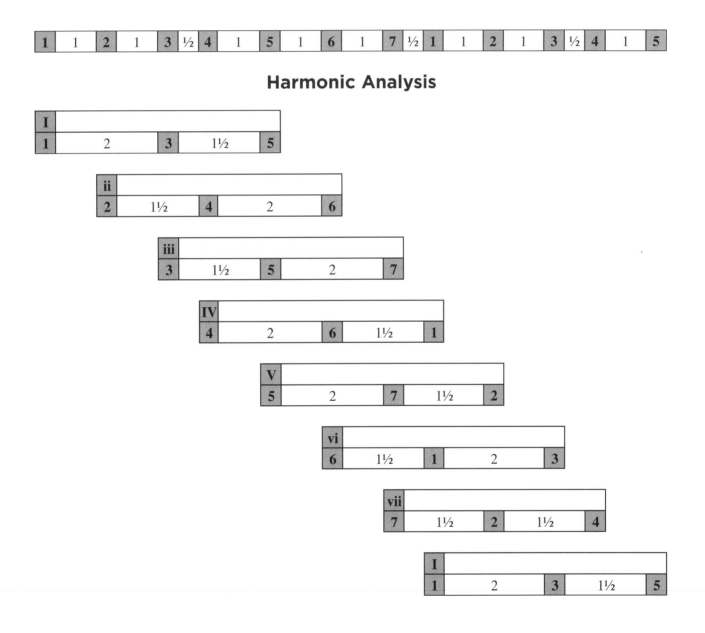

Harmonic Analysis

Ionian Set Triad Studies

Three-tone chords, otherwise called *triads*, may be applied in a melodic as well as a harmonic context.

Major and minor triads are unique in that they are the only two triads consisting of exclusively *consonant* intervals:

1. Minor Third, *ideal frequency ratio 6/5*
2. Major Third, *ideal frequency ratio 5/4*
3. Perfect Fourth, *ideal frequency ratio 4/3*
4. Perfect Fifth, *ideal frequency ratio 3/2*
5. Minor Sixth, *ideal frequency ratio 8/5*
6. Major Sixth, *ideal frequency ratio 5/3*

Also: Perfect Unison, *ideal frequency ratio 1/1*, and the Perfect Octave, *ideal frequency ratio 2/1*.

The table below shows the relationships of the intervals within these two triads:

Major Triad (close position)

C	Root	
		} Perfect Fourth
G	Fifth	
		} Minor Third
E	Third	
		} Major Third
C	Root	

Minor Triad (close position)

C	Root	
		} Perfect Fourth
G	Fifth	
		} Major Third
E♭	Third	
		} Minor Third
C	Root	

Major Triad (open position)

C	Root	
		} Minor Sixth
E	Third	
		} Major Sixth
G	Fifth	
		} Perfect Fifth
C	Root	

Minor Triad (open position)

C	Root	
		} Major Sixth
E♭	Third	
		} Minor Sixth
G	Fifth	
		} Perfect Fifth
C	Root	

figure 29

Because of the inclusion of only consonant intervals, these two triads are considered special for use in substitutions and extensions. Eleven other useful triads may be found as subsets of four-tone chords which may be applied in a melodic as well as a harmonic context.

Ionian Set Modal Cadences and Progressions

When choosing to compose in the realms of the modes of the Ionian set, care must be taken to remain within the constraints of the current mode. While non-diatonic notes (chromatic approach tones, etc) may be used in the melody or when soloing over the changes, the majority of melody notes (and <u>all</u> of the harmony notes) will always be drawn from the pool of the seven diatonic notes contained in the current mode.

Modal compositions and sections (as opposed to major and "composite minor" tonal works) must clearly define the tonic chord. This is usually done by establishing the tonic before moving on to any other chord.

It is not always necessary to introduce <u>all</u> seven diatonic notes of a mode into the melody or harmony in order to establish its "mood" (qv. "ModeChords" in the appendices pg 161). It is, however, imperative that the *characteristic notes* (one or the other of the tritone components, and usually the quality-defining third as well) be explicitly included somewhere in either the melody or harmony to firmly establish the mode's true identity and to avoid ambiguity.

If the melody does not contain the characteristic notes of the mode in question, then the harmony is responsible for defining the quality and character of the relevant mode; and if the harmony is ambiguous, then the melody must be the defining factor.

Modal chord motions, cadences and progressions tend to be quite simple. Often they use basic triadic structures. While 7th, 9th and even 11th chords and suspensions can also be used for color, as with all functional harmony, <u>the most important factor is root motion</u>.

While it is certainly possible to regard modal chords as being either *"tonic or non-tonic"*, not all non-tonic chords are equal. This chapter is primarily concerned with the relative cadential strengths of the motions from the various non-tonic chords back to their tonic (and these chords' uses in modal progressions).

In major and "composite minor" tonal progressions, the chord with the strongest need to resolve to the tonic is called the *"dominant"* and is built off the fifth degree of the scale.

In modal progressions, the chords that strongly need to resolve to the tonic are sometimes called *"modal dominants"*, but they are usually <u>not</u> built off the fifth degree. Consequently, the term *"cadential chord"* will be used throughout here to avoid any confusion.

Below are the general guidelines to determining the degree of a chord's cadential strength in modal contexts (in order of importance):

1. **Proximity of the non-tonic chord's root to the tonic root**

   a) step-wise cadences

   In tonal cadences, the most typical cadential motion is circular (approaching the tonic root by ascending or descending fourths or fifths).

   In modal cadences, however, the most typical and strongest cadential motions are step-wise (approaching the tonic root by ascending or descending a whole-step or half-step).

   b) circular motions

   One of the reasons that circular progressions are somewhat less common in modal situations is because introducing circular chord motion tends to lead one down a slippery slope that can strongly gravitate towards the parent ionian's tonic.

   However, the V-I and IV-I motions still can and do occur in modal cadences and progressions, even though they are not as powerful in the modal context as the step-wise cadences.

   c) movement by thirds

   Approaching the tonic root by ascending or descending thirds (m3 or M3) is not usually considered cadential in either tonal or modal cadences (rather they are felt as simply a "change of color"). As such, chords whose roots are a third away from the tonic root are generally considered "non-cadential chords" (the one exception being the ♭VI-i cadence in the Aeolian mode).

2. **Chord quality**

   Chords containing a major third yield a stronger cadential feel than those containing a minor third.

3. **Presence of the characteristic note**

   While the presence of the characteristic note is certainly a plus to giving a chord more cadential strength in a modal setting, factors #1 and #2 above (root proximity and chord quality) tend to carry more weight.

4. **Avoidance of the diminished triad**

   Since the tritone of the diminished triad exerts such a strong tendency to resolve to the root and major third of its parent Ionian scale, it is typically avoided (the exceptions being in certain Aeolian cadences or when occurring in a chord as a non-functional color tone, as in the m6 chords and blues 7ths).

Modal Chord Functions:
Primary Cadential, Secondary Cadential, Non-Cadential and Pre-Cadential

In the case of tonal cadences, the *"primary cadential chord"* (ie. the chord with the *"strongest need to resolve to the tonic"*) is the dominant V chord (or its tritone substitute).

The best examples of *"secondary cadential chords"* in a tonal context are the subdominant and its substitutions (ie. the chord yielding the *"second strongest resolution to the tonic"* – not to be confused with *"secondary dominant"*).

As is seen below, each mode may possess several cadential chords (both primary and secondary), as well as *"non-cadential chords"* (those chords without a cadential tendency) and *"avoid chords"* (a chord whose tendencies point <u>away</u> from the modal tonic).

Pre-Cadential Chords

In tonal musics, there exist *"pre-dominant chords."* This genre represents a chord in a progression which immediately *"<u>precedes</u> the <u>dominant</u> chord."*

Two common examples of pre-dominant chords in tonal musics are the ii (or II) as in the ii-V-I progression, and the ♭VI (or ♭vi) as in the ♭VI-V-I progression.

In the case of modal progressions, these chord functions are termed here as *"pre-cadential chords."* While these pre-cadential chords may also be cadential chords in their own right, they are equally as likely to be non-cadential chords.

Chord sequences come in three basic varieties:

1. Oscillation: Alternating between a tonic chord and a non-tonic cadential chord.

2. Progression: A sequence of chords gravitating towards a resolution to a tonic.

3. Succession: A sequence of unrelated non-functional-harmony chords not progressing towards a tonic. There exists an infinite number of chord successions, and since they have no bearing on this current discussion there will be no further mention of them here.

Oscillation between the tonic and a non-tonic chord is often considered to be a static harmony. However, it should be noted that when the non-tonic chord is being played, the melody most often consists of its chord tones. Which reflects and reinforces the components of the underlying non-tonic chord, adding a sense of direction and motion to the melody line.

Progressions consisting of a root motion *"turn"* (eg. I-II-I-VII-I or I-VII-I-II-I) and those consisting of a *"surrounding note figure"* approach ("SNF" aka "encirclement" or "enclosure") (eg. I-VII-II-I or I-II-VII-I) can both be thought of as *"extended oscillations"* (especially considering that in the case of the SNF the pre-cadential chord and the cadential chord are simply "third substitutes" of each other).

While tonal progressions tend to follow circular motions (or variations of circular motions via substitutions), modal progressions have more latitude.

Just as stepwise motion yields the strongest cadential feel in modal cadences, a stepwise motion from a pre-cadential chord to the cadential chord yields a strong progression terminating in a satisfying and "final" resolution to the modal tonic.

In addition to stepwise motions, the cadential chord can be approached either via circular motion (up or down a perfect fifth or perfect fourth), or be preceded by its substitute chord a third away (up or down a M3 or m3).

In the following sections, each individual mode is examined along with a discussion of the relative strength of its cadential chords; examples of typical modal progressions and the use of pre-cadential chords in those progressions.

The Locrian mode has not been included here because it is so rarely used as a center of tonality.

Phrygian Cadences and Progressions

The Phrygian is identical to the "pure minor" scale (Aeolian) except for its characteristic note: *the ♭2*. The tonic triad is minor, and the tonic tetrad is a minor 7th.

It should be noted that in many Spanish styles of music, the tonic minor is replaced by the parallel tonic major chord, and common scales to play over this "Phrygian" tonic major are the "Phrygian dominant scale" [1 ♭2 **3** 4 5 ♯5(♭6) ♭7] (the 5th mode of the harmonic minor), the octatonic "Spanish Phrygian" (aka *"Phyrgian add ♮3"*) [1 b2 ♭3 ♮**3** 4 5 ♭6 ♭7] (3rd mode of the bebop major scale), and the Superphrygian (*Phrygian ♭4*) [1 ♭2 ♭3 **M3(♭4)** 5 ♯5(♭6) ♭7] (3rd mode of the harmonic major).

Phrygian Triads	Phrygian Tetrads
Primary Cadential Chord	Primary Cadential Chord
♭II	♭IImaj7
Secondary Cadential Chords	Secondary Cadential Chords
♭viim ivm	♭viim7 ivm7
Non-Cadential Chords	Non-Cadential Chord
♭III ♭VI	♭VImaj7
Avoid Chord	Avoid Chords
v°	♭III7 vØ7

♭II

The resolution ♭II-I is the strongest cadence in the phrygian. It contains all of the elements that constitute a powerful modal cadential chord: step-wise motion (down a half-step), it is a major quality chord and it contains the characteristic note in its root.

♭IImaj7

The addition of a major 7th to this chord does nothing to alter its cadential strength. The major 7th here simply adds color.

♭viim

This is the relative minor of the primary cadential chord. Its strong points are that its root is a whole-step away from the tonic root and that it contains the characteristic note, as well as its substitutive relationship with the primary cadential ♭II chord. Its weak point is its minor third.

♭viim7

The addition of a ♭7 to this chord adds to its cadential strength as it is the 5th of its relative ♭II cadential chord (♭viim7 is the enharmonic equivalent of ♭II6) and due the ♭7's voice leading tendency to resolve to the 5th of the Phrygian tonic chord.

ivm

This chord's only strength is its IV-I plagal root motion. Its weaknesses are that it contains a minor third and does not contain the characteristic note. In addition, since the iv-i motion also exists in the Aeolian, it can be ambiguous in the absence of other characteristic elements.

ivm7

The addition of a ♭7 to this chord does nothing to alter its cadential strength. The ♭7 here simply adds color.

♭III

This chord is the relative major of the phrygian minor tonic. Its root is a minor third away from the tonic root and it does not contain the characteristic note. Motion to and from this chord to the Phrygian tonic is not felt as a cadence, rather a "change of color". In addition, since the ♭III-i motion also exists in the Aeolian and Dorian, it can be ambiguous in the absence of other characteristic elements.

♭III7

The addition of a ♭7 to this chord adds in the characteristic note. However, the tritone in this dominant chord exhibits a strong tendency to resolve to the parent ionian's tonic and in most situations is best avoided.

♭VI

This chord is the tonic of the parent Ionian. Its root is a major third away from the tonic root and it does not contain the characteristic note. In addition, since the ♭VI-i motion also exists in the aeolian, it can be ambiguous in the absence of other characteristic elements.

♭VImaj7

The addition of a major 7th to this chord does nothing to alter its cadential strength. The major 7th here simply adds color.

v°

As in most other modes, the tendency of the tritone in this triad so strongly needs to resolve to the parent Ionian's root and third that it is avoided.

vØ7

As in most other modes, the tendency of the tritone in this tetrad so strongly needs to resolve to the parent Ionian's root and third that it is avoided.

Examples of Phrygian Cadences and Progressions

(The "I" chord may be substituted for the "i")

1. i ♭II i   (oscillation)

2. i ♭viim7 i   (oscillation)

3. i ivm i   (oscillation)

4. i ♭viim7 i ♭IImaj7 i   (turn)

5. i ♭IImaj7 i ♭viim7 i   (turn)

6. i ♭viim7 ♭IImaj7 i   (SNF)

7. i ♭IImaj7 ♭viim7 i   (SNF)

8. i ♭III ♭IImaj7 i   (stepwise/stepwise)

9. i ♭VImaj7 ♭viim7 i   (stepwise/stepwise)

10. im im7/♭7 ivm7 ♭IImaj7 im   (3rd/stepwise)

11. i ♭VImaj7 ♭IImaj7 i   (circle/stepwise)

12. i ivm7 ♭viim7 i   (circle/stepwise)

13. i ♭III/5 ♭viim7 i   (circle/stepwise)

13. i ♭IImaj7 ivm i   (3rd sub/circle)

14. i ♭viim7 ivm i   (circle/circle)

15. i ♭IImaj7 ♭III ♭IImaj7 i   (extended)

16. im im7/♭7 ♭VImaj7 ivm7 ♭IImaj7 im   (extended)

Aeolian Cadences and Progressions

The aeolian is also known as the "natural minor" or "pure minor" scale. It differs from the Ionian scale in that it contains a ♭3, a ♭6 and a ♭7. Since the Dorian and Phrygian also contain both a ♭3 and a ♭7, its characteristic note is *the ♭6*. The tonic triad is minor, and the tonic tetrad is a minor 7th.

Aeolian Triads	Aeolian Tetrads
Primary Cadential Chord	Primary Cadential Chord
♭VII	♭VII7
Secondary Cadential Chords	Secondary Cadential Chords
ivm vm ii° ♭VI	ivm7 vm7 iiØ7 ♭VImaj7
Non-Cadential Chord	Non-Cadential Chord
♭III	♭IIImaj7

♭VII

The resolution ♭VII-i is the strongest cadence in the aeolian, and the most common. Its strengths are: stepwise motion (up a whole-step – "gamma cadence") and that it is a major quality chord. Its weaknesses are that it doesn't contain the characteristic note, and also since the ♭VII-i cadence exists in the Dorian, it can be ambiguous in the absence of other characteristic elements.

The ♭VII-i (or ♭VII-I) cadence is one of the three strongest cadences in music, and is also known as the *"gamma cadence"* (with the *"alpha cadence"* being the V-I root motion, and the *"beta cadence"* being the IV-I root motion).

♭VII7

The presence of the ♭7 here adds in the characteristic note, thereby strengthening the already strong cadential feel of this chord motion in the Aeolian.

Care must be taken, though, with this chord as it also has a strong tendency to want to resolve to the tonic of the parent Ionian.

ivm

This is also a common cadential chord in the Aeolian. Its main strengths are that it possesses the characteristic note and has the plagal iv-i root motion. Its weakness is the presence of the minor third.

ivm7

The addition of a ♭7 to this chord does nothing to alter its cadential strength. The ♭7 here simply adds color.

vm

This is another common cadential chord in the Aeolian. Its only strength is its v-i motion. Its weaknesses are the lack of the characteristic note and the presence of the minor third.

In addition, since the v-i motion also exists in the Dorian, it can be ambiguous in the absence of other characteristic elements.

vm7

The addition of a ♭7 to this chord does nothing to alter its cadential strength. The ♭7 here simply adds color.

ii°

As long as the relative major (the tonic of the parent Ionian) is not referenced in close proximity, this can be a very strong cadential chord in the aeolian.

This is due not only to the fact that its root is a whole-step above the Aeolian root, but also because the tritone formed with its root and ♭5 needs to resolve to the m3rd and 5th of the Aeolian tonic minor.

iiØ7

The addition of a ♭7 to this chord does nothing to alter its cadential strength. The ♭7 here simply adds color.

♭VI

This chord's strengths are that it contains both a major third and the characteristic note. Its weakness is that its root is a major third away from the aeolian tonic root. In addition, since the ♭VI-i motion also exists in the Phrygian, it can be ambiguous in the absence of other characteristic elements.

♭VImaj7

The addition of a major 7th to this chord does nothing to alter its cadential strength. The major 7th here simply adds color.

♭III

This chord is the relative major of the Aeolian minor tonic as well as the tonic of the parent Ionian. Motion to and from this chord to the Aeolian tonic is not felt as a cadence, rather a "change of color".

In addition, since the ♭III-i motion also exists in the Dorian and Phrygian, it can be ambiguous in the absence of other characteristic elements.

♭IIImaj7

The addition of a major 7th to this chord does nothing to alter its cadential strength. The major 7th here simply adds color.

Examples of Aeolian Cadences and Progressions

1. im ♭VII im   (oscillation)

2. im ♭VII7sus im   (oscillation)

3. im ii° im   (oscillation)

4. im vm im   (oscillation)

5. im ivm im   (oscillation)

6. im ♭VI im   (oscillation)

7. im7 iim7♭5 im7 ♭VII7 im7   (turn)

8. im7 ♭VII7 im7 iim7♭5 im7   (turn)

9. im7 iim7♭5 ♭VII7 im7   (SNF)

10. im7 ♭VII ii° im7   (SNF)

11. im im7/♭7 ♭VImaj7 ♭VII7 im7   (stepwise/stepwise)

12. im7 ♭IIImaj7 iim7♭5 im7   (stepwise/stepwise)

13. im7 vm7 ♭VII7 im7   (3rd/stepwise)

14. im7 ivm7 iim7♭5 im7   (3rd/stepwise)

15. im7 ♭VImaj7 iim7♭5 im7   (tritone/stepwise)

16. im7 vm7 ii° im7   (circle/stepwise)

17. im im7/♭7 ivm7 ♭VII7 im7   (circle/stepwise)

18. im7 ♭IIImaj7 ♭VII7 im7   (circle/stepwise)

19. im7 ivm7 vm7 im7   (stepwise/circle)

20. im im7/♭7 ♭VImaj7 ivm7 im7   (3rd sub/circle)

21. im7 ♭VII vm7 im7   (3rd sub/circle)

22. im7 ♭IIImaj7 vm7 im7   (3rd sub/circle)

23. im7 ♭VImaj7 vm7 im7   (stepwise/circle)

24. im7 vm7 ivm7 im7   (stepwise/circle)

25. im7 ♭IIImaj7 ivm7 im7   (stepwise/circle)

26. im7 ♭VImaj7 vm7 im7   (stepwise/circle)

27. im7 ♭VII ivm7 im7   (circle/circle)

28. im7 vm7 ♭VImaj7 im7   (stepwise/3rd)

29. im7 ♭VII(add 9) ♭VImaj7 im7   (stepwise/3rd)

30. im7 ivm7 ♭VImaj7 im7   (3rd sub/3rd)

31. im7 ♭IIImaj7 ♭VImaj7 im7   (circle/3rd)

32. im ♭VII ♭VI ♭VII im   (extended)

33. im7 ♭VImaj7 vm7 ivm7 im7   (extended)

34. im7 ♭VImaj7 vm7 ivm7 ♭IIImaj7 ivm7 im7 (extended)

35. im7 ivm7 im7 ii° im7   (mixed)

36. im7 ivm7 im7 ♭VII im7   (mixed)

Dorian Cadences and Progressions

The Dorian is identical to the "pure minor" scale (aeolian) except for its characteristic note: *the M6*. The tonic triad is minor, and the tonic tetrad can be either a minor 7th or a minor 6th.

Dorian Triads	Dorian Tetrads
Dorian Triads	**Dorian Tetrads**
Primary Cadential Chord ♭VII	Primary Cadential Chord ♭VIImaj7
Secondary Cadential Chords IV iim vm	Secondary Cadential Chords IV7 iim7 vm7
Non-Cadential Chord ♭III	Non-Cadential Chord ♭IIImaj7
Avoid Chord vi°	Avoid Chord viØ7

♭VII

The resolution ♭VII-i is the strongest cadence in the Dorian, yet not the most common. Its strengths are: stepwise motion (up a whole-step – "gamma cadence") and that it is a major quality chord. Its weaknesses are that it doesn't contain the characteristic note, and also since the ♭VII-i cadence is the most common cadential motion in the aeolian, it can be ambiguous in the absence of other characteristic elements.

♭VIImaj7

The addition of a major 7th introduces the characteristic note into this chord strengthening its already strong cadential feel.

IV

This is the most common cadential chord in dorian. Its strengths are a IV-i plagal root motion, that it is a major chord, and the presence of the characteristic note (its 3rd).

IV7

The addition of the ♭7 here doesn't alter its cadential strength. In fact, the IV7-i is one of the most common Dorian cadences. The ♭7 here adds color, but care must be taken that a ii-V7-I progression leading towards the parent Ionian is not implied.

iim

This chord's strengths are its proximity to the tonic root (whole-step above) and the presence of the characteristic note (its 5th). Its weakness is its m3.

iim7

The addition of a ♭7 to this chord does nothing to alter its cadential strength. The ♭7 here simply adds color.

vm

The vm can also used as a cadential chord in the Dorian. Its only strength lies in its v-i motion. Its weaknesses are that it does not contain the characteristic note, and that it possesses a minor 3rd.

In addition, since the v-i motion also exists in the Aeolian, it can be ambiguous in the absence of other characteristic elements.

vm7

The addition of a ♭7 to this chord strengthens its cadential feel as it is the relative minor substitute for the strong cadential ♭VII chord.

♭III

This chord is the relative major of the dorian minor tonic. Motion to and from this chord to the Dorian tonic is not felt as a cadence, rather a "change of color". In addition, since the ♭III-i motion also exists in the Aeolian and Phrygian, it can be ambiguous in the absence of other characteristic elements.

♭IIImaj7

The addition of a major 7th to this chord does nothing to alter its cadential strength. The major 7th here simply adds color.

vi°

As in most other modes, the tendency of the tritone in this triad so strongly needs to resolve to the parent Ionian's root and third that it is avoided.

viØ7

As in most other modes, the tendency of the tritone in this tetrad so strongly needs to resolve to the parent Ionian's root and third that it is avoided.

Examples of Dorian Cadences and Progressions

1. im7   iim7   im7   (oscillation)

2. im7   IV7   im7   (oscillation)

3. im7   ♭VIImaj7   im7   (oscillation)

4. im7   vm7   im7   (oscillation)

5. im7   ♭VIImaj7   im7   iim7   im7   (turn)

6. im7   iim7   im7   ♭VIImaj7   im7   (turn)

7. im9   iim7   ♭VIImaj7   im9   (SNF)

8. im7   ♭VIImaj7   iim7   im7   (SNF)

9. im7   ♭IIImaj7   iim7   im7   (stepwise/stepwise)

10. im7   vm7   ♭VIImaj7   im7   (3rd sub/stepwise)

11. im   IV   iim7   im   (3rd sub/stepwise)

12. im7   IV   ♭VIImaj7   im7   (circle/stepwise)

13. im7   ♭IIImaj7   ♭VIImaj7   im7   (circle/stepwise)

14. im7   vm7   iim7   im7   (circle/stepwise)

15. im   iim   IV   im   (3rd sub/circle)

16. im7   ♭VIImaj7   vm7   im7   (3rd sub/circle)

17. im9   vm9   IV9   im9   (stepwise/circle)

18. im7   ♭IIImaj7   IV7   im7   (stepwise/circle)

19. im7   IV   vm7   im7   (stepwise/circle)

20. im7   ♭VIImaj7   IV   im7   (circle/circle)

21. im7   iim7   vm7   im7   (circle/circle)

22. im7   iim7   ♭IIImaj7   IV   im   (composite)

23. im7   iim7   ♭IIImaj7   iim7   im7   (composite)

Mixolydian Cadences and Progressions

The Mixolydian is identical to the Ionian scale except for its characteristic note: *the ♭7*. The tonic triad is major, and the tonic tetrad can be either a dominant 7th, a sus7 or a (major) 6th.

When using the tonic dominant 7th tetrad, it is often treated as a "Blues 7th chord", where the ♭7 forms a non-functional tritone with its M3 and is simply a "color" note.

Mixolydian Triads	Mixolydian Tetrads
Primary Cadential Chord ♭VII	**Primary Cadential Chord** ♭VIImaj7
Secondary Cadential Chords vm iim IV	**Secondary Cadential Chords** vm7 iim7 IVmaj7
Non-Cadential Chord vim	**Non-Cadential Chord** vim7
Avoid Chord iii°	**Avoid Chord** iiiØ7

♭VII

The resolution ♭VII-I is the strongest cadence in the Mixolydian. It contains all of the elements that constitute a powerful modal cadential chord: stepwise motion (up a whole-step – "gamma cadence"), it is a major quality chord and it contains the characteristic note in its root.

♭VIImaj7

The addition of a major 7th to this chord does nothing to alter its cadential strength. The major 7th here simply adds color.

vm

This is also a common choice for a cadential chord in the Mixolydian. Its strengths are the presence of the characteristic note, a v-I root motion, and its substitutive relationship with the primary cadential ♭VII chord. Its weakness is its m3.

vm7

The addition of a ♭7 to this chord adds to its cadential strength as it is the 5th of its relative ♭VII cadential chord (vm7 is the enharmonic equivalent of ♭VII6), and due to the ♭7's voice leading tendency to resolve to the 3rd of the Mixolydian tonic chord (which parallels the strong "Isus4 – I major" resolution).

Care must be taken, however, with the order of the other chords in the progression to insure that the vm7 - I cadence in the Mixolydian is not perceived as a iim7 - V motion leading to the parent Ionian.

iim

This chord's main strength is its proximity to the tonic root (whole-step above). Its weaknesses are its m3 and lack of characteristic note. Yet, in spite of those shortcomings, it is still capable of yielding a solid cadential feel due to its substitutive relationship with the primary cadential ♭VIImaj7 tetrad.

iim7

The addition of a ♭7 to this chord does nothing to alter its cadential strength. The ♭7 here simply adds color.

IV

The IV may also be used as a cadential chord in the Mixolydian. Its strengths lie in its IV-I plagal resolution (as paralleled in the major), and its M3 component. Its weaknesses are that it does not contain the characteristic note, and that it is also the tonic of the parent Ionian.

While it can be used convincingly as a cadential chord, care must be taken with the order of the other chords in the progression not to imply that the tonic of the Mixolydian is actually the V of the parent Ionian.

IVmaj7

The addition of a major 7th to this chord does nothing to alter its cadential strength. The major 7th here simply adds color.

vim

This chord is the relative minor of the Mixolydian tonic. Motion to and from this chord to the Mixolydian tonic is not felt as a cadence, rather a "change of color".

vim7

The addition of a ♭7 to this chord does nothing to alter its cadential strength. The ♭7 here simply adds color.

iii°

As in most other modes, the tendency of the tritone in this triad so strongly needs to resolve to the parent Ionian's root and third that it is avoided.

iiiØ7

As in most other modes, the tendency of the tritone in this tetrad so strongly needs to resolve to the parent Ionian's root and third that it is avoided.

Examples of Mixolydian Cadences and Progressions

1. I ♭VII I   (oscillation)

2. I vm7 I   (oscillation)

3. I7sus iim7 I7sus   (oscillation)

4. I ♭VIImaj7 I iim7 I   (turn)

5. I iim7 I ♭VIImaj7 I   (turn)

6. I iim7 ♭VII(add 9) I(add 9)   (SNF)

7. I ♭VIImaj9 iim7 I   (SNF)

8. I vim ♭VII I   (stepwise/stepwise)

9. I7sus vm7 ♭VIImaj7 I   (3rd sub/stepwise)

10. I vm7 iim7 I   (circle/stepwise)

11. I IVsus ♭VIImaj7 I   (circle/stepwise)

12. I ♭VII/2 vm7 I   (3rd sub/circle)

13. I vm7 IVsus I   (stepwise/circle)

14. I IVmaj7 vm7 I   (stepwise/circle)

15. I vim7 vm7 I   (stepwise/circle)

16. I ♭VIImaj7 IVmaj7 I   (circle/circle)

17. I iim7 vm7 I   (circle/circle)

18. I ♭VII vim ♭VII I   (extended)

19. I vm vim ♭VII I   (extended)

20. I ♭VII(add 9) vim7 vm7 I   (extended)

Ionian Modal Cadences and Progressions

In the tonal major, the strongest cadence is the V-I (or V7-I) motion. However, the Ionian can be used as a purely modal non-dominant harmony system via the avoidance/splitting of the tritone, the avoidance of dominant resolutions, the use of stepwise cadences and motions, etc.

Therefore, when treating the Ionian as a pure modal (versus tonal major) construct, its characteristic note is the *P4*. The tonic triad is major, and the tonic tetrad is most typically a major 7th, but can also be a (major) 6th chord.

Ionian Triads	**Ionian Tetrads**
Primary Cadential Chord	Primary Cadential Chord
iim	iim7
Secondary Cadential Chords	Secondary Cadential Chords
IV iiim*	IVmaj7 iiim7*
Non-Cadential Chords	Non-Cadential Chords
vim iiim*	vim7 iiim7*
Avoid Chords	Avoid Chords
V vii°	V7 viiØ7

iim

The resolution iim-I is the strongest cadence in the Ionian modal system. Its strengths are its step-wise motion (down a whole-step), and that it contains the characteristic note as its third. Its weakness is its m3.

iim7

The addition of a ♭7 to this chord does nothing to alter its cadential strength. The ♭7 here simply adds color.

IV

This chord's strengths are that it is a major chord, and that it contains the characteristic note as its root. Its weakness (vis-a-vis the iim cadential chord) is its IV-I motion (as paralleled in the tonal major),

IVmaj7

The addition of a maj7 to this chord does nothing to alter its cadential strength. The maj7 here simply adds color.

vim

This chord is the relative minor of the ionian tonic. Motion to and from this chord to the Ionian tonic is not felt as a cadence, rather a "change of color".

vim7

The addition of a ♭7 to this chord does nothing to alter its cadential strength. The ♭7 here simply adds color.

*iiim

This chord's root is a major third away from the tonic root, it possesses the weak minor third and it does not contain the characteristic note. Oscillation to and from this chord to the Ionian tonic is not felt as a cadence, rather a "change of color" (ie. as a rootless tonic maj7 chord).

In addition, since the iiim-I motion also exists in the Lydian, it can be ambiguous in the absence of other characteristic elements.

As the iiim is the relative minor substitute of the tonal major's dominant chord, it contains both the tonal dominant's root as its third and the tonal major's leading tone as its fifth. Due to its leading tone it can be used as a "soft" cadential chord when preceded by a pre-cadential chord.

*iiim7

The addition of a ♭7 to this chord does nothing to alter its cadential strength. The ♭7 here simply adds color. However, since the iiim7 is enharmonically identical to the V6, it can imply a tonal major V-I cadential feel.

V

By definition, a non-dominant harmony system avoids the dominant-tonic motion.

V7

The tendency of the tritone in this tetrad so strongly needs to resolve to the tonal major's root and third, that this dominant-tonic motion is avoided in a pure modal setting.

vii°

The tendency of the tritone in this triad so strongly needs to resolve to the tonal major's root and third, that this dominant-tonic motion is avoided in a pure modal setting.

viiØ7

The tendency of the tritone in this tetrad so strongly needs to resolve to the tonal major's root and third, that this dominant-tonic motion is avoided in a pure modal setting.

Examples of Ionian Modal Cadences and Progressions

1. I   iim   I   (oscillation)

2. I   IV   I   (oscillation)

3. Imaj7   iim7   Imaj7   (oscillation)

4. Imaj7   IVmaj7   Imaj7   (oscillation)

5. Imaj7   iiim7   iim7   I   (stepwise/stepwise)

6. I maj7   vim7   iim7   Imaj7   (circle/stepwise)

7. Imaj7   IVmaj7   iim7   Imaj7   (3rd sub/stepwise)

8. Imaj7   iiim7   IVmaj7   Imaj7   (stepwise/circle)

9. Imaj7   iim7   IVmaj7   Imaj7   (3rd sub/circle)

10. Imaj7   vim7   IVmaj7   Imaj7   (3rd sub/circle)

11. Imaj7   iim7   iiim7   IVmaj7   Imaj7   (extended)

12. Imaj7   IVmaj7   iiim7   iim7   Imaj7   (extended)

13. Imaj7   iim7   iiim7   Imaj7   (stepwise/3rd)

14. Imaj7   IVmaj7   iiim7   Imaj7   (stepwise/3rd)

15. Imaj7   vim7   iiim7   Imaj7   (circle/3rd) [also exists in Lydian]

16. IVmaj7   iiim7   iim7   Imaj7   (extended)

Lydian Cadences and Progressions

The Lydian is identical to the Ionian scale except for its characteristic note: *the #4*. The tonic triad is major, and the tonic tetrad is most typically a major 7th, but can also be a maj7♭5(#4) or a (major) 6th.

Lydian Triads	Lydian Tetrads
Primary Cadential Chord	**Primary Cadential Chord**
II	*II**
Secondary Cadential Chords	Secondary Cadential Chords
viim V iiim**	viim7 Vmaj7 iiim7**
Non-Cadential Chords	Non-Cadential Chords
vim iiim**	vim7 iiim7**
Avoid Chord	Avoid Chords
#iv°	#ivØ7 II7*

II

The resolution II-I is the strongest cadence in the Lydian. It contains all of the elements that constitute a primary modal cadential chord: step-wise motion (down a whole-step), it is a major quality chord and it contains the characteristic note as its third.

*II7

The II7's tritone's tendency to resolve to the parent Ionian's major tonic make it a rarity in Lydian progressions. Most typically, <u>only the II major triad is used as the primary cadential chord in the Lydian</u>.

viim

This is the relative minor of the primary cadential chord. Its strong points are that its root is a half-step away from the tonic root and that it contains the characteristic note. Its weak point is its minor third.

viim7

The addition of a ♭7 to this chord does nothing to alter its cadential strength. The ♭7 here simply adds color.

V

This chord's strengths are its V-I motion (as paralleled in the major), and that it is a major chord. Its weakness is its lack of characteristic note.

In addition, since it is the tonic of the parent Ionian, care must be taken with the order of the other chords in the progression not to imply that the tonic of the Lydian is actually the IV of the parent Ionian.

Vmaj7

The presence of a major 7th here adds in the characteristic note, strengthening the cadence somewhat in the Lydian context. Care must still be taken, though, with the order of the other chords in the progression not to imply that the tonic of the Lydian is actually the IV of the parent Ionian.

vim

This chord is the relative minor of the Lydian tonic. Motion to and from this chord to the Lydian tonic is not felt as a cadence, rather a "change of color".

vim7

The addition of a ♭7 to this chord does nothing to alter its cadential strength. The ♭7 here simply adds color.

**iiim

This chord's root is a major third away from the tonic root, it possesses the weak minor third and it does not contain the characteristic note. Oscillation to and from this chord to the Lydian tonic is not felt as a cadence, rather a "change of color." In addition, since the iii-I motion also exists in the Ionian, it can be ambiguous in the absence of other characteristic elements.

As the iiim is the relative minor substitute of the V chord, it contains the leading tone as its fifth. Due to the presence of this leading tone it can be used as a "soft" cadential chord when preceded by a pre-cadential chord.

**iiim7

The addition of a ♭7 to this chord does nothing to alter its cadential strength. The ♭7 here simply adds color. However, since the iiim7 is enharmonically identical to the V6, it can imply a V-I cadential feel.

#iv°

As in most other modes, the tendency of the tritone in this triad so strongly needs to resolve to the parent Ionian's root and third that it is avoided.

#ivØ7

As in most other modes, the tendency of the tritone in this tetrad so strongly needs to resolve to the parent Ionian's root and third that it is avoided.

Examples of Lydian Cadences and Progressions

1. I II I   (oscillation)

2. I viim I   (oscillation)

3. I Vmaj7 I   (oscillation)

4. Imaj7 viim7 Imaj7 II Imaj7   (turn)

5. Imaj7 II Imaj7 viim7 Imaj7   (turn)

6. Imaj7 viim7 II Imaj7   (SNF)

7. Imaj7 II viim7 Imaj7   (SNF)

8. Imaj7 iiim7 II Imaj7   (stepwise/stepwise)

9. Imaj7 vim7 viim7 Imaj7   (stepwise/stepwise)

10. Imaj7 iiim9 viim7 Imaj7   (circle/stepwise)

11. Imaj7 vim7 II Imaj7   (circle/stepwise)

12. Imaj7 viim7 Vmaj7 Imaj7   (3rd sub/circle)

13. Imaj7 iiim7 Vmaj7 Imaj7   (3rd sub/circle)

14. Imaj7 vim7 Vmaj7 Imaj7   (stepwise/circle)

15. Imaj7 II Vmaj7 Imaj7   (circle/circle)

16. I II iiim II I   (extended)

17. I viim vim viim I   (extended)

18. Imaj7 II iiim7 Imaj7   (stepwise/3rd)

19. Imaj7 viim7 iiim7 Imaj7   (circle/3rd)

20. Imaj7 vim7 iiim7 Imaj7   (circle/3rd) [also exists in Ionian]

The Derivation of Radially Symmetrical Altered Scales

Central Point of Reference
D

1st Level
The Quartal Consonants of D [A and G]

4th   4th
<u>A</u>   **D**   **<u>G</u>**
(figure 30)

2nd Level
Add quartal consonants of A and G [E and C]

4th   4th   4th   4th
<u>E</u>   **A**   **D**   **G**   **<u>C</u>**
(figure 31)

the minor pentatonic scale
A   **C**   **D**   **E**   **G**
(figure 32)

3rd Level
Add quartal consonants of E and C [B and F]

4th   4th   4th   4th   4th   4th
<u>B</u>   **E**   **A**   **D**   **G**   **C**   **<u>F</u>**
(figure 33)

the minor scale
A   **B**   **C**   **D**   **E**   **F**   **G**
(figure 34)

The Major Scale
C   **D**   **E**   **F**   **G**   **A**   **B**
(figure 35)

Level 4

Taking this law of 4ths (as in figures 31 and 33 on page 40) another step further,
we now have the following 9-pitch group:

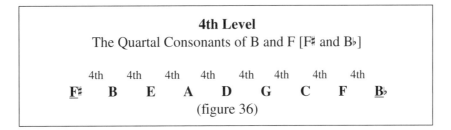

4th Level

The Quartal Consonants of B and F [F♯ and B♭]

4th	4th	4th	4th	4th	4th	4th	4th
F♯	B	E	A	D	G	C	F	B♭

(figure 36)

By substituting both of the two new notes for their natural namesakes
(B becomes B♭ and F becomes F♯),
we arrive at a this radially symmetrical 7-note structure:

A   B♭   C   D   E   F♯   G

(figure 37)

Rearranged (similar to page 40 figure 34 above),
this yields what is commonly known as
the G melodic minor scale:

melodic minor scale

G   A   B♭   C   D   E   F♯

(figure 38)

This scale's modes are quite common and very useful
(Lydian augmented scale, Lydian dominant scale, altered scale, etc)

Level 5

Taking the logic of outwardly-radiating 4ths the next step further,
we now have the following 11-pitch set:

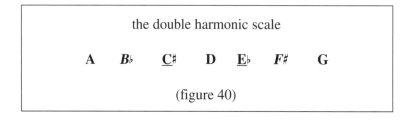

5th Level
Quartal Consonants of F♯ and B♭ [C♯ and E♭]

4th	4th	4th	4th	4th	4th	4th	4th	4th	4th

C♯   F♯   B   E   A   D   G   C   F   B♭   E♭

(figure 39)

Level 5a

Preserving Level 4's B♭ and F♯,
substitute both of the two new notes C♯ and E♭ for their natural namesakes,
(C becomes C♯, E becomes E♭)
and we arrive at this eastern 7-note scale:

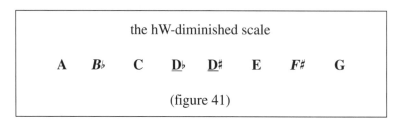

the double harmonic scale

A   B♭   C♯   D   E♭   F♯   G

(figure 40)

Level 5b

Preserving Level 4's B♭ and F♯,
substitute both the enharmonic notes D♭ and D♯ for the D,
and we arrive at the most common of all 8-note scales:

the hW-diminished scale

A   B♭   C   D♭   D♯   E   F♯   G

(figure 41)

Our central focus of radial symmetry has been D.

In the diminished scale, both D♭ and D♯ are one half-step equidistant from the primary axis of symmetry D.

Level 5c

Neutralizing Level 4's B♭ and F♯ alterations, (B♭ reverts to B, F♯ reverts to F)
substitute the new notes C♯/D♭ and the D♯/E♭
for all of their natural namesakes,
(both C and D become C♯/D♭, and both D and E merge to become D♯/E♭)
and we arrive at this 6-note scale:

---

the wholetone scale

A   **B**   **C♯/D♭**   **D♯/E♭**   **F**   **G**

(figure 42)

Level 6

Taking the final quartal step,
we now have the following 13(12)-pitch set:

6th Level
Quartal Consonant of C♯ and E♭ [G♯/A♭]

	4th	4th	4th	4th	4th	4th	4th	4th	4th	4th	4th	4th
G♯	**C♯**	**F♯**	**B**	**E**	**A**	**D**	**G**	**C**	**F**	**B♭**	**E♭**	**A♭**

(figure 43)

THE CHROMATIC SCALE

Level 6a

Preserving Level 4's B♭ and F♯,
and also using Level 5♭'s alterations (D♭ and D♯),
substitute the new A♭/G♯ for both the A and the G.
Yielding this 8(7) note scale:

A♭ **B♭** **C** **D♭** **D♯** **E** **F♯** **G♯**

(figure 44)

---

rearranged and enharmonically spelled:

C♯/D♭ melodic minor scale

D♭	E♭	F♭	G♭	A♭	B♭	C
C♯	D♯	E	F♯	G♯	A♯	B♯

(figure 45)

Level 6b

Neutralizing Level 5♭'s D♭ and D♯ alterations
(D♭ reverts to D, and D♯ reverts to D)
while preserving Level 4's alterations (B♭ and F♯),
yields this 7(6) note pitch set:

---

the wholetone scale

A♭   **B♭**   **C**   **<u>D</u>**   **E**   **F♯**   **G♯**

(figure 46)

Level 6c

Preserving Level 4's B♭ and F♯,
and using Level 5c's alterations (C♯/D♭ and D♯/E♭ for C, D, and E),
we arrive this 6(5) note scale:

A♭   **B♭**   **<u>C♯/D♭</u>**   **<u>D♯/E♭</u>**   **F♯**   **G♯**

(figure 47)

---

rearranged and enharmonically spelled:

D♯/E♭ minor pentatonic

E♭	**G♭**	**A♭**	**B♭**	**D♭**
D♯	**F♯**	**G♯**	**A♯**	**C♯**

(figure 48)

Level 6d

As in 6c above, preserving Level 4's B♭ and F♯,
and using Level 5c's alterations (C♯/D♭ and D♯/E♭ for C, D, and E),
but also allowing in the natural B and natural F from the third level,
we arrive this 8(7) note scale:

A♭	B♭	B	C♯/D♭	D♯/E♭	F	F♯	G♯

(figure 49)

enharmonically spelled:

A♭/G♯ Dorian mode

A♭	B♭	C♭	D♭	E♭	F	G♭	A♭
G♯	A♯	B	C♯	D♯	E♯	F♯	G♯

(figure 50)

Level 6e

Neutralizing all of Level 4's and Level 5's alterations,
and allowing in a natural A and a natural G from the first level,
we arrive at this 9(8) note scale:

G♯	<u>A</u>	B	C	D	E	F	<u>G</u>	A♭

(figure 51)

rearranged:

the bebop major scale

C	D	E	F	G	A♭/G♯	A	B

(figure 52)

46

Within all of the above radially symmetrical scales
(minor and major pentatonic scales; Ionian set modes;
double harmonic scale; the melodic minor modes; wholetone scales;
the diminished scales and the bebop major scale)
are found every practical chord possibility.

These results are all obtained by
using extremely basic laws of physics and
strict logic **in only six short steps**.

As a footnote to this discussion of radially symmetrical scales, it is interesting to note that whenever symmetrical scales are mentioned in traditional theory books, only the wholetones and diminisheds are the ones to get any press.

Check out all these other common scales that are also *symmetrical*.

The minor pentatonic is radially symmetrical in two ways:

A minor pentatonic
A   C   **D**   E   G
m3 W I W m3

D♯/E♭ minor pentatonic
A♭ B♭ D♭ I D♯ F♯ G♯
W   m3   **W**   m3   W

**The modes of the natural scale (ionian set)
are also radially symmetrical in two ways:**

A Aeolian
A   B   C   **D**   E   F   G
W   h   W I W   h   W

A♭ Dorian
A♭ B♭ C♭ D♭ I E♭ F G♭ A♭
W   h   W   **W**   W   h   W

And the Jazz Minor is radially symmetrical in two ways:

G Jazz Minor
A B♭ C **D** E F♯ G
h   W   W I W   W   h

C♯/D♭ Jazz Minor
A♭ B♭ C D♭ I D♯ E F♯ G♯
W   W   h   **W**   h   W   W

Dorian Centric Alterations

When creating altered scales by substituting one "accidental" at a time, the Dorian has ability to generate the largest number (4) of distinct scale families out of all of the seven ionian sets.

There is only one way to stack fifths to arrive at "D Dorian" with the point of origin being "D" and that is by stacking the fifths radiating outwards from the central D.

figure 53

The Pythagorean intervals generated by successive fifths,
both upwards and downwards:

ratios **8/27 4/9 2/3 1/1 3/2 9/4 27/8** F   C   G   **D**   A   E   B
without adjusting the ranges **1/1 9/4 8/27 2/3 3/2 27/8 4/9 (2/1)** D   E   F   G   A   B   C   (D)
with ratios adjusted to fit all the notes within the range of one octave **32/27 16/9 4/3 1/1 3/2 9/8 27/16** F   C   G   D   A   E   B
in ascending order reduced to a single octave: **1/1 9/8 32/27 4/3 3/2 27/16 16/9 (2/1)** D   E   F   G   A   B   C   (D)

figure 54

Since we are dealing with an outwardly radiating stack of fifths here, let's first examine those "accidentals" that radiate upwards from the highest "natural stacked fifth" B:

D E F G A B C substitute **F♯** = D E **F♯** G A B C = "Mixolydian Scale" (5th mode of Ionian)

D E F G A B C substitute **C♯** = D E F G A B **C♯** = "Jazz Minor (root position)"

D E F G A B C substitute **G♯** = D E F **G♯** A B C = "Harmonic Minor Scale" (4th mode)

Next, those fifths radiating downwards from the lowest "natural stacked fifth" F

D E F G A B C substitute **B♭** = D E F G A **B♭** C = "Aeolian Scale" (6th mode of Ionian)

D E F G A B C substitute **E♭** = D **E♭** F G A B C = "Jazz Minor" (2nd mode)

D E F G A B C substitute **A♭** = D E F G **A♭** B C = "Harmonic Major Scale" (2nd mode)

figure 55

D E F **G♯** A B C
D E F G A B **C♯**
D E **F♯** G A B C

axis — D E F G A B C — axis

D E F G A **B♭** C
D **E♭** F G A B C
D E F G **A♭** B C

figure 56

NB: Substituting the G♯ yields the Harmonic Minor, but substituting the A♭ yields the Harmonic Major. Which are both sub-sets of the "Dorian Blues" scale.

The Minor Scales

This chapter deals with the following 4 minor scales: Dorian, Aeolian, harmonic minor, and ascending melodic minor (for this chapter the "ascending melodic minor" is referred to as "melodic minor").

The **Dorian** mode is composed of two minor tetrachords stacked on top of one another.

The **Aeolian** mode is composed of a minor tetrachord on the bottom and a Phrygian tetrachord on the top. The Aeolian is also known as the "natural minor".

The **Harmonic** Minor has a minor tetrachord on the bottom, and a harmonic tetrachord on the top.

The Harmonic Minor has an exotic sound due to the ♯2 interval between its 6th and 7th degrees. This is one of the principal scales used in Arabic, Gypsy and Spanish musics.

The **Melodic** Minor has a minor tetrachord on the bottom, and a major tetrachord on the top.

You'll note that every one of the above scales has in common the minor tetrachord on the bottom. In fact the bottom FIVE notes are the same in all of them.

(The A minor pentachord is: A B C D E)

The only differences between these scales are the qualities of the 6ths and 7ths.

Natural Minor Modes vs. Altered Minor Scales

The "natural minor modes" here are the Dorian and Aeolian. They are termed "natural" because they can be constructed beginning from the 2nd (Dorian) and 6th (Aeolian) degrees of the major scale.

The <u>Dorian</u> has the minor pentachord on the bottom, its 6th is a major 6th interval from the root and the 7th is a minor 7th interval from the root.

The <u>Aeolian</u> differs from the Dorian in only one respect - it has a ♭6.

Note that the 7th degree of EITHER natural minor mode is a minor 7th interval from the root (♭7). That is to say that a ♭7 is the normal 7th for natural minor modes.

The "altered minor scales" differ very little from the "natural minor scales". One feature both these scales have in common is the raised 7.

The <u>harmonic minor</u> differs from the Aeolian in only one respect - it has a raised 7.

The <u>melodic minor</u> differs from the harmonic minor in only one respect - it has a maj6 instead of a ♭6.

The Dorian differs from the melodic minor in only one respect - it has the ♭7 instead of a raised 7th.

Comparison of Minor Scales Table

Dorian Formula:
R-W-h-W-W-**W**-**h**-W

Aeolian Formula:
R-W-h-W-W-**h**-**W**-W

Dorian Degrees:
1 2 ♭3 4 5 **6** ♭**7**

Aeolian degrees:
1 2 ♭3 4 5 **b**♭ ♭**7**

Dorian example in A:
A B C D E **F♯** **G** A

Aeolian example in A:
A B C D E **F** **G** A

Melodic Minor formula:
R-W-h-W-W-**W**-**W**-h

Harmonic Minor Formula:
R-W-h-W-W-**h**-**♯2**-h

Melodic Minor Degrees:
1 2 ♭3 4 5 **6** **7**

Harmonic Minor Degrees:
1 2 ♭3 4 5 ♭**6** **7**

Melodic Minor example in A:
A B C D E **F♯** **G♯** A

Harmonic Minor example in A:
A B C D E **F** **G♯** A

figure 57

Interchangeability

One can choose (relatively freely) which type of 6ths and which type of 7ths you'd like to use (depending on your intent).

Combining the four above scales yields the minor pentachord on the bottom and all the chromatics between the 5th and the octave. In other words - a nine-note scale. The chordal analyses in the appendix (pgs 142-156) construct chords off of each of these nine scale degrees.

No chords are constructed from the ♯4/♭5 degree, but it is very common to use this tone when improvising as:

a) a leading tone into the 5th,

b) a blue note,

c) a very interesting passing tone.

That gives us a 10-note scale that we can use to improvise over minor chords and minor progressions. We only avoid the ♭2 (which would put us into Phrygian) and the M3 (which would put us into major).

Natural Minor Harmony
vs.
Borrowed Parallel Major Harmony

In pure modal tonal centers, the chords tend to be triads or at most 7th chords. The harmonic sequences are generally simple and repetitive.

The function of the "cadential chord" (the second most important chord in the key) is to propel you into the tonic. In major harmony, the chord with the most forceful resolution to the tonic is built off the fifth of the scale ("dominant V").

In the case of the **Dorian** and **Aeolian** modal harmony, the dominating cadential chord is typically built off the 4th and ♭7th degrees respectively.

The harmonic minor provides a leading tone to give a stronger cadence than either the Dorian IV > i or Aeolian ♭VII > i movements yield (via "borrowed parallel major harmony").

Often entire sections of a tune will use Aeolian, and the only time the harmonic minor comes into play is whenever a "dominant V chord" resolution is needed.

Hence the term "harmonic" minor - it is a non-symmetrical scale designed to aid the <u>harmonic</u> accompaniment.

The harmonic minor scale leaves some folks uneasy with the ♯2 "big jump" between the ♭6 and the 7. **The melodic minor** smoothes over the ♯2 jump and is "more melodic". Hence the term "<u>melodic</u> minor".

Note that the only difference between the melodic minor and its parallel major scale is that the melodic minor has a ♭**3**.

Major Scale
1 2 <u>**3**</u> 4 5 6 7

Melodic Minor Scale
1 2 ♭<u>**3**</u> 4 5 6 7

figure 58

Since many contemporary musics generally deal more with "borrowed parallel major harmony" than pure modal harmony, this chapter's tables in the appendix (pages 142 thru 156) reflect circle-based tonal gravity.

The Broken Circle

While major harmony resolves itself nicely around the circle of 4ths, minor circles have a little "kink" in them.

In addition, depending on which minor scale we have chosen to base our composition on, there can be several options.

The following table illustrates the tonal gravity root movement inherent in minor chord progressions (gravitating towards the tonic minor at the bottom of the table):

Circular Minor Chord Sequences Table
(read from top to bottom)

IV	
♭VII	
♭III	VI
♭VI	II
	V or ♮VII
	I

figure 59

IV → ♭VII → ♭III → ♭VI   OR   IV → ♭VII → VI → ♭VI

IV → ♭VII → ♭III → II   OR   IV → ♭VII → VI → II

As can be seen, a neat circular sequence is not possible. Note, however, that the ♭**III and VI are tritone substitutes for one another**, as are the ♭**VI and II** chords.

For the dominant function, it's possible to use chords built off the fifth degree OR chords built off the raised 7th degree.

II → V → I   or   II → ♮VII → I

♭VI → V → I   or   ♭VI → ♮VII → I

For an example of how the above table can be used to construct a tune, compare the root movement in this section of *"Autumn Leaves"* to the table above:

| **IV** | ♭**VII** | ♭**III** | ♭**VI** | **II** | **V** | **I** | **I** |

figure 60

Melodic Materials

Of interest to composers and improvisers are these scales (derived from radially symmetrical structures) most commonly used in occidental musics:

1) The pentatonic scales (major and minor)

2) The whole-tone scale (hexatonic)

3) The major scale and its modes (heptatonic)

4) The jazz minor scale and its modes (heptatonic)

5) The diminished scales (octatonic)

6) The Dorian blues scale (octatonic) and its two non-symmetrical heptatonic subsets:
    a) The harmonic minor scale
    b) The harmonic major scale

These eight scales are of great interest, since one may navigate the complexities of most chord progressions and implied harmonic environments by applying these scales *in the simplest way possible*. A huge percentage of current and past musics may be reduced to but a few simple guidelines.

This does not eliminate other scales and pitch sets from consideration; it will be demonstrated how to apply these most common pitch sets in such a way as to eliminate the need for cumbersome terminology.

Harmonic Environments

Of import to the composer and improviser are the various types of harmonic environments that may be encountered. Here the terms "real" and "unreal" are used. Take for example the following standard jazz progression:

Fm7 - B♭m7 - E♭7 - A♭maj7 - D♭maj7 - G7 - Cmaj7

Instead of classical analysis, which for some progressions proves to be unwieldy, the process is simplified by choosing local or global analyses:

Local (chord by chord)
(works best for slower tempos and/or longer forms)

Real Chords

An example of applying melody to real chords is the classic chord/scale theory approach where the F Aeolian is played over the Fm7, B♭ Dorian over B♭m7, E♭ Mixolydian over the E♭7, A♭ Lydian over the A♭maj7, G Mixolydian over the G7 and C Lydian over the Cmaj7.

Unreal Chords

Unreal chords are applied by deriving melodic material from chords not actually played. For example, it is common to use D♭7 instead of G7 as a tritone substitution; therefore, a D♭ Mixolydian scale may be applied to the G7 chord even though a D♭7 isn't actually being played.

Global (key center)
(established via major or minor progressions and resolutions, etc)

Real Keys

Real keys are established by conventional modal and tonal harmonic progressions, such as the vi - ii - V7 - I (Fm7 - B♭m7 - E♭7 - Abmaj7) progression as well as the V7 - I (G7 - Cmaj7) resolution. The vi - ii - V7 - I in A♭ indicates the key of A♭ major and the V7 - I in C indicates the key of C major.

Unreal Keys

Unreal keys are perhaps the most "outside" sounds to be had in chromatic theory. In this context, playing in an "unreal" key refers to key centers not evidenced by the underlying harmony itself. Soloing devices in this category include, but are not be limited to, techniques such as side-slipping.

The Chromatic Modes

This section represents the culmination of many years of analyses and study into the subjects of modality and symmetry. The common practices of both composition and improvisation give rise to a great many scales and chords, along with many methods to describe them.

Terms like "half-whole diminished" and "altered dominant" may be well established as part and parcel of the modern musician's vocabulary; however, here it is hoped to avoid fuzzy definitions wherever possible.

This solution to the dilemma is simple. Although it *is* necessary to introduce some non-conventional terminology in order to properly describe the phenomena, an idiom is developed here that is simple, elegant, and intuitive.

The logical path requires an examination of first the modes themselves, followed by an expansion of the basic major scale into its most commonly used variations.

The major scale has seven modes. The jazz minor also has seven modes. That's fourteen. Include the harmonic minor modes, diminished, and whole-tone scales now. The diminished scale has only two modes and the whole-tone has but one; adding in the modes of the harmonic major scale, makes a total of **31** modes (7+7+7+7+2+1) that you are required to remember.

Traditional lists of modes and scales are too large. What has been developed here may be of benefit; therefore, a step-by-step method is provided to bridge the communication gap.

First of all, it has been shown that all scales may be ultimately derived from the central "D" of the A natural minor cum basic major scale. Secondly, it follows that modes of all other scales are similarly available, again as variations of the basic major scale modes.

Using radial symmetry, it is demonstrated how ALL scales may be derived from the simplest of concepts. This does not eliminate the need for serious study and practice for true musicianship; however, the conceptualization of the symmetries between the various scales involved may make some of your practice routine more logical.

Chromatic Modes

The major scale may be broken down into seven modes. Examples are given here with the parent scale of C major:

C   D   E   F   G   A   B   C

1) C Ionian

C   D   E   F   G   A   B   C

2) D Dorian

D   E   F   G   A   B   C   D

3) E Phrygian

E   F   G   A   B   C   D   E

4) F Lydian

F   G   A   B   C   D   E   F

5) G Mixolydian

G   A   B   C   D   E   F   G

6) A Aeolian

A   B   C   D   E   F   G   A

7) B Locrian

B   C   D   E   F   G   A   B

The true character of the modes becomes apparent when transposing them to start on the same tonic note:

C Ionian (I$^\Delta$ of C major)

C	D	E	F	G	A	B	C

C Dorian (ii of B♭ major)

C	D	E♭	F	G	A	B♭	C

C Phrygian (iii of A♭ major)

C	D♭	E♭	F	G	A♭	B♭	C

C Lydian (IV$^\Delta$ of G major)

C	D	E	F♯	G	A	B	C

C Mixolydian (V^7 of F major)

C	D	E	F	G	A	B♭	C

C Aeolian (vi of E♭ major)

C	D	E♭	F	G	A♭	B♭	C

C Locrian (vii$^\emptyset$ of D♭ major)

C	D♭	E♭	F	G♭	A♭	B♭	C

To further understand the sounds of the modes, they may be arranged in order of "brightness," with the Lydian being the "brightest" and the Locrian being the "darkest," with Dorian at the "mid-point."

C Lydian

| C | D | E | F♯ | G | A | B | C |

C Ionian

| C | D | E | F | G | A | B | C |

C Mixolydian

| C | D | E | F | G | A | B♭ | C |

C Dorian

| C | D | E♭ | F | G | A | B♭ | C |

C Aeolian

| C | D | E♭ | F | G | A♭ | B♭ | C |

C Phrygian

| C | D♭ | E♭ | F | G | A♭ | B♭ | C |

C Locrian

| C | D♭ | E♭ | F | G♭ | A♭ | B♭ | C |

Note that the seven modes above with C as the tonic represent the seven major scales in which the C is present:

G major, C major, F major, B♭ major, E♭ major, A♭ major, and D♭ major

Since the Circle of Fifths has been already established from the most sharps to the least sharps, the remaining major scales (which do not contain the note C) are listed below in a similar order:

F♯ major

F♯	G♯	A♯	B	C♯	D♯	E♯	F♯

B major

B	C♯	D♯	E	F♯	G♯	A♯	B

E major

E	F♯	G♯	A	B	C♯	D♯	E

A major

A	B	C♯	D	E	F♯	G♯	A

D major

D	E	F♯	G	A	B	C♯	D

Playing the aforementioned major scales over a C bass creates five chromatic modes in addition to the original seven modes of the Ionian set:

I	Ionian	(in C: a C major scale over a C bass)
♭II	Pseudo-altered	(in C: a B major scale over a C bass)
II	Dorian	(in C: a B♭ major scale over a C bass)
♭III	Pseudo-Lydian ♯5	(in C: an A major scale over a C bass)
III	Phrygian	(in C: an A♭ major scale over a C bass)
IV	Lydian	(in C: a G major scale over a C bass)
♭V	Pseudo-Locrian	(in C: a G♭ major scale over a C bass)
V	Mixolydian	(in C: an F major scale over a C bass)
♭VI	Aug-dim	(in C: an E major scale over a C bass)
VI	Aeolian	(in C: an E♭ major scale over a C bass)
♭VII	Pseudo-Lydian	(in C: a D major scale over a C bass)
VII	Locrian	(in C: a D♭ major scale over a C bass)

figure 61

Although the seven modes of the ionian set have a rich and diverse history regarding their use and function in melody and harmony, the five "chromatic modes" do not. The following tables show in greater detail how one might use the chromatic modes in actual practice.

Since the bass note of the five chromatic modes is not included in the scale, the scale may be altered to produce the most closely related major, minor, jazz minor, harmonic major or harmonic minor scales. This alteration is not necessary, but is often desirable in order to produce a familiar scale and sonority.

Other interpretations are, in fact, possible and it is hoped that the reader will investigate these concepts further to their logical conclusions. All of the seven Ionian set modes and the five "chromatic modes" are collectively referred to here as the *"Twelve Chromatic Modes"*.

Chromatic Modes with Inversions

1st chromatic mode

one • **Ionian**
    ◦ **Primary Horizontal Major**

1	2	3	4	5	6	7

inversion 1   Major Chords in Second Inversion

5	[6]	7	1	[2]	3	[♯4]

inversion 2   minor chords in third inversion

♭7	1	[2]	♭3	[4]	5	[6]

2nd chromatic mode

flat two • **Pseudo-altered**
    ◦ **Altered Dominant**

[1]	♭2	♭3	♭4	♭5	♭6	♭7

↳ *root has been altered to incorporate the related jazz minor scale*

3rd chromatic mode

two • **Dorian**
    ◦ **minor**

1	2	♭3	4	5	6	♭7

inversion 3   minor chords in root position

1	[2]	♭3	[4]	5	[6]	♭7

inversion 4   half-diminished chords in first inversion

♭3	[4]	♭5	[♭6]	♭7	1	[♭2]

inversion 5   Dominant Chords in Second Inversion

5	[6]	♭7	1	[2]	3	[4]

4th chromatic mode

flat three • **Pseudo-Lydian ♯5**
    ◦ **Altered Major**

[1]	2	3	♯4	♯5	6	7

↳ *root has been altered to incorporate the related jazz minor scale*

5th chromatic mode

three • **Phrygian**

○ **secondary horizontal minor**

1	♭2	♭3	4	5	♭6	♭7

○ **Dominant to minor**

5	♭6	♭7	1	2	♭3	4

inversion 6   Major Chords in Third Inversion

7	1	[2]	3	[♯4]	5	[6]

6th chromatic mode

four • **Lydian**

○ **Major**

1	2	3	♯4	5	6	7

inversion 7   Major Chords in Root Position

1	[2]	3	[♯4]	5	[6]	7

inversion 8   minor chords in first inversion

♭3	[4]	5	[6]	♭7	1	[2]

inversion 9   half-diminished chords in second inversion

♭5	[♭6]	♭7	1	[2]	♭3	[4]

inversion 10   Dominant Chords in Third Inversion

♭7	1	[2]	3	[4]	5	[6]

7th chromatic mode

flat five • **Pseudo-Locrian**

[1]	♭2	♭3	4	♭5	♭6	♭7

↳ *root has been altered to incorporate the related Major scale*

---

circle shift : sharp direction

see also : 12th chromatic mode (seven) and inversions 15-16

8th chromatic mode

five • **Mixolydian**

○ **Secondary Horizontal Major**

1	2	3	4	5	6	♭7

○ **Dominant to Major**

5	6	7	1	2	3	4

inversion 11   Dominant Chords in Root Position

1	[2]	3	[4]	5	[6]	♭7

9th chromatic mode

flat six
- augmented-diminished scale
  - ◦ diminished / Augmented

[1]	♭2		♯2/♭3	3/♭4		♯4/♭5		♯5/♭6		6/d7		7

↳ *root is altered to incorporate the related Harmonic Major and minor scales*

10th chromatic mode

six
- Aeolian
  - ◦ primary horizontal minor

1		2	♭3		4		5	♭6		♭7

inversion 12   Major Chords in First Inversion

3		[♯4]	5		[6]		7	1		[2]

inversion 13   minor chords in second inversion

5		[6]	♭7		1		[2]	♭3		[4]

inversion 14   half-diminished chords in third inversion

♭7		1	[♭2]		♭3		[4]	♭5		[♭6]

11th chromatic mode

flat seven
- Pseudo-Lydian

[1]		2		3		♯4	5		6		7

↳ *root has been altered to incorporate the related Major scale*

---

circle shift : flat direction

see also : 6th chromatic mode (four) and inversions 7-10

12th chromatic mode

seven
- Locrian
  - ◦ half-diminished

1		♭2		♭3		4	♭5		♭6		♭7

inversion 15   half-diminished chords in root position

1		[♭2]		♭3		[4]	♭5		[♭6]		♭7

inversion 16   Dominant Chords in First Inversion

3		[4]		5		[6]	♭7		1		[2]

The Chromatic Cube

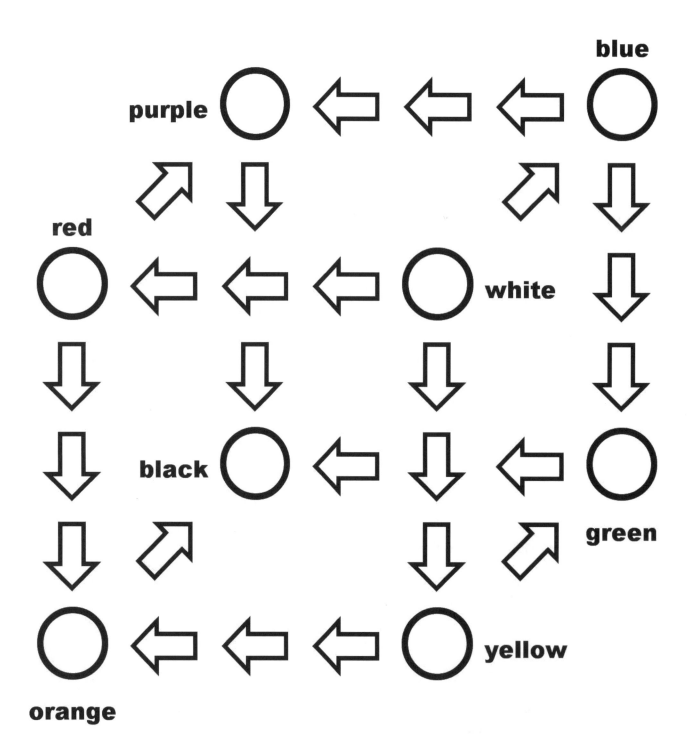

In order to demonstrate the relationships that exist between the most common radially symmetrical musical scales (hexatonic, heptatonic and octatonic), eight colors are used here:

White, Red, Orange, Yellow, Green, Blue, Purple, and Black

Tones of a chromatic nature (existing outside the basic major scale) are assigned colors; it is as simple as that. The result is that we will be using terms that are intuitive and familiar.

To begin with, the radially symmetrical heptatonic ur-scale (the natural scale) has the least amount of tension *(no color)* and is therefore simply referred to as White:

Natural Scale = White
A   B   C   D   E   F   G

Modes of this scale are well established as being associated with certain chords, primarily:

$$Am7 \quad B^{Ø7} \quad C^{\Delta} \quad Dm7 \quad Em7 \quad F^{\Delta} \quad G7$$

In addition to the lesser used, but important nonetheless, chords of the chromatic modes:

$$B\flat^{\Delta} \quad C\sharp^{7\sharp5} \quad E\flat^{\Delta\sharp5} \quad F\sharp^{Ø} \quad G\sharp^{\circ(\sharp5)}$$

Once a key has been established for a musical situation (ie. a chord, a tonality, a mode, a resolving tendency of one or more chords, etc…), any scale related to the parent Ionian scale may be used to provide color. Here's how it works:

Let's say that the second mode of the familiar C Ionian scale has been established during a Dorian groove such as Dm7 G7:

$$D \quad E \quad F \quad G \quad A \quad B \quad C \quad D$$

The first alteration that may be applied here is the melodic minor scale generated by raising the C to C♯:

$$D \quad E \quad F \quad G \quad A \quad B \quad C\sharp \quad D$$

The above pitch set could be called:

- C major scale with a raised root (C♯ Superlocrian), or
- D jazz minor, or
- G Lydian dominant (referencing the G7♯11 chord)

But here, it is simply called: "Red."

C♯ = Red

The C♯ is referred to as the "Red Component" and the scales generated by this alteration (D melodic minor, etc) are also referred to as "Red."

The first tone of the C Ionian mode has been raised in order to provide a D minor major seventh, or a jazz minor context to the D minor chord (while at the same time augmenting the fourth/eleventh of the G7th chord).

Similarly, the second color is the melodic minor scale generated by lowering the E to E♭:

D　E♭　F　G　A　B　C　D

This could be called:

- C major scale with a lowered third, or
- C jazz minor, or
- D Dorian ♭2, or
- G Mixolydian ♭6 (referencing the G7♭13 chord)

Here it is simply called: "Yellow."

E♭ = Yellow

The E♭ is the yellow component and the scales generated by this alteration (C jazz minor, etc) are also christened, "Yellow."

Here the language is greatly simplified by removing (temporarily) the lengthy terminologies that are often used to define what are essentially very simple chromatic alterations.

These two colors distinguish two chromatic variations from the basic C major scale (White), which yields three scales:

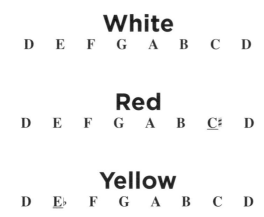

White

D   E   F   G   A   B   C   D

Red

D   E   F   G   A   B   <u>C♯</u>   D

Yellow

D   <u>E♭</u>   F   G   A   B   C   D

Substituting both the C♯ (red component) and the E♭ (yellow component) simultaneously, or "red" + "yellow," yields "orange:"

<u>E♭</u>   F   G   A   B   <u>C♯</u>

C♯ (Red) + E♭ (Yellow) = Orange

Here the D has been "split" [**D♭** ⇦ D ⇨ **D♯**] to provide the familiar hexatonic whole-tone scale.

So far four colors have been introduced. These are the "bright" colors: white, red, orange, and yellow. The next four are the "dark" colors.

Introducing the G♯/A♭ into the "White scale" yields the octatonic **D Dorian blues scale**:

D   E   F   G   <u>G♯/A♭</u>   A   B   C   D

This is called "Blue" and the G♯/A♭ is the blue component:

G♯/A♭ = Blue

The Dorian blues scale is a very diverse pitch set as many commonly used scales can be derived from it:

A Harmonic Minor Scale
(heptatonic)

A   B   C   D   E   F   G♯   A

C Harmonic Major Scale
(heptatonic)

C   D   E   F   G   A♭   B   C

D Minor Blues Scale
(hexatonic)

D   F   G   A♭   A   C   D

C Bebop Major Scale
(octatonic)

C   D   E   F   G   A♭   A   B   C

E Spanish Phyrgian Scale
(octatonic)

E   F   G   G♯   A   B   C   D   E

A Bebop Harmonic Minor Scale
(octatonic)

A   B   C   D   E   F   G   G♯   A

The G♯/A♭ is "Blue," as are the scales generated by this alteration (D Dorian blues, A harmonic minor, C harmonic major, D minor blues, C bebop major, E Spanish Phrygian, A bebop harmonic minor, etc).

A further application of the Blue (G♯/A♭) note is to split the fifth of the D melodic minor Red scale to produce this familiar octatonic diminished scale:

D E F G <u>A♭</u> <u>A♯</u> B <u>C♯</u> D

Note that the C♯ (the red component) is present along with the blue component (A♭), hence the name: "purple."

A♭ (Blue) + C♯ (Red) = Purple

The split fifth has produced one new note, the A♯ which is here called the "purple component" because it is unique to the "purple scale."

Splitting the fifth of the C melodic minor (yellow – E♭) scale produces this diminished scale

C D <u>E♭</u> F <u>G♭</u> <u>G♯</u> A B C

to yield the green (blue + yellow) scale:

E♭ (Yellow) + G♯ (Blue) = Green

The split fifth of the C melodic minor scale has produced one new note, the G♭ and is here called the "green component" because it is unique to the "green scale."

Finally, the "black scale" is introduced by applying ALL colors simultaneously. The B and F remain as "essential tones" along with red (C♯/D♭), blue (G♯/A♭), yellow (D♯/E♭), green (G♭/F♯), and purple (A♯/B♭) to produce:

Black

C♯	D♯	E♯(F)	F♯	G♯	A♯	B
D♭	E♭	F	G♭	A♭	B♭	C♭(B)

The black G♭ major scale represents the most "outside" color that may be applied to the harmonic environments found in music. It is the tritone substitution/complement of the original natural C white heptatonic ur-scale and thus shares very little of its sonority.

Radial Symmetry – The Bright Colors

Shown on page 73 is the symmetry exhibited by the "brightest" colors of the chromatic cube. Once the parent Ionian scale has been chosen, the other chromatic modes may be used to color the basic melodic and harmonic choices.

For example, let's say that a melody is being played over

Dm G7 CΔ

the most obvious choice for the parent scale is C Ionian.

If one were to apply the "red scale" to the G7 chord, the effect would be to augment the 4th (or 11th) of the chord, yielding the D melodic minor (fourth mode):

G   A   B   C♯   D   E   F   G

If the yellow were used over the G7, the flatted sixth is present

G   A   B   C   D   E♭   F   G

which is the C melodic minor scale (fifth mode).

Further, if the "orange scale" were used on the G7, notice that it is the G9♯5 (whole-tone) scale:

G   A   B   C♯   E♭   F   G

The concept of symmetry may be used to greatly simplify the choices used by the performer.

Jazz chord/scale theory would have labeled two of these choices for the G7 chord as "Lydian dominant" and "Mixolydian ♭6" where all that has been done here is to simply refer to them as "red" and "yellow."

No attempt is being made here to replace the rich and diverse historical traditions of the development and application of melodic materials. Rather, these observations are meant to point out the simplicity in melodic choices that has always existed.

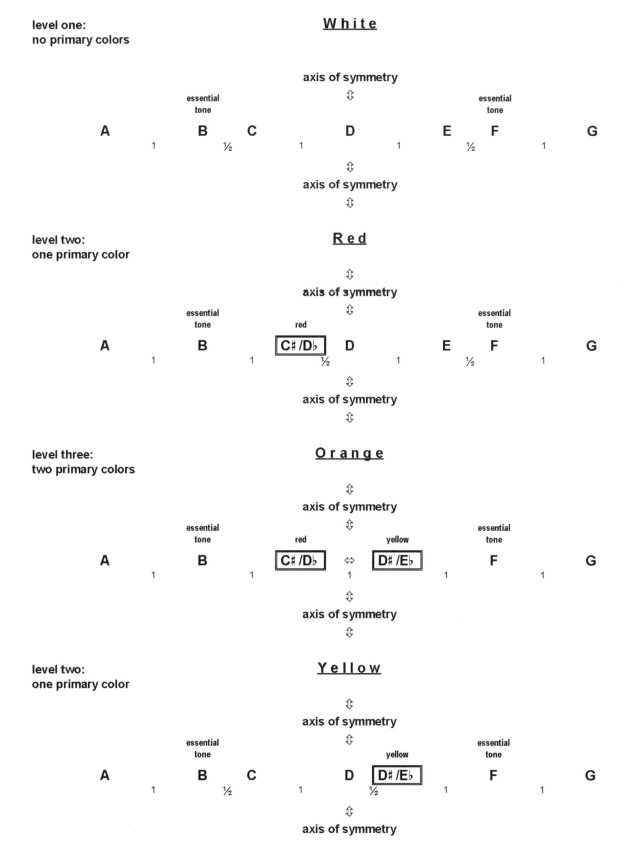

Radial Symmetry – The Dark Colors

Shown on page 75 is the symmetry exhibited by the "darkest" colors of the chromatic cube. Once the parent Ionian scale has been chosen, its other chromatic modes may be used to color the basic melodic and harmonic choices.

Once again, say that a melody is being played over

Dm G7 CΔ

the most obvious choice for the parent scale is C Ionian.

Applying the octatonic "blue scale" to the C chord, the effect is to produce the C bebop major scale:

C   D   E   F   G   G♯   A   B   C

If the "purple scale" is used over G7, it yields the half-whole diminished scale:

G   A♭   B♭   B   C♯   D   E   F   G

Further, if the "black scale" (G♭ Ionian) is used in this context, notice how the tritone substitute of G Mixolydian (D♭ Mixolydian) appears:

D♭   E♭   F   G♭   A♭   B♭   C♭   D♭

Applying the "red" alteration to the "black scale" (raising the root of G♭ Ionian) yields the G Superlocrian scale (aka G alt scale / G dim-WT scale / G Locrian ♭4 scale)

G   A♭   B♭   C♭   D♭   E♭   F   **G**

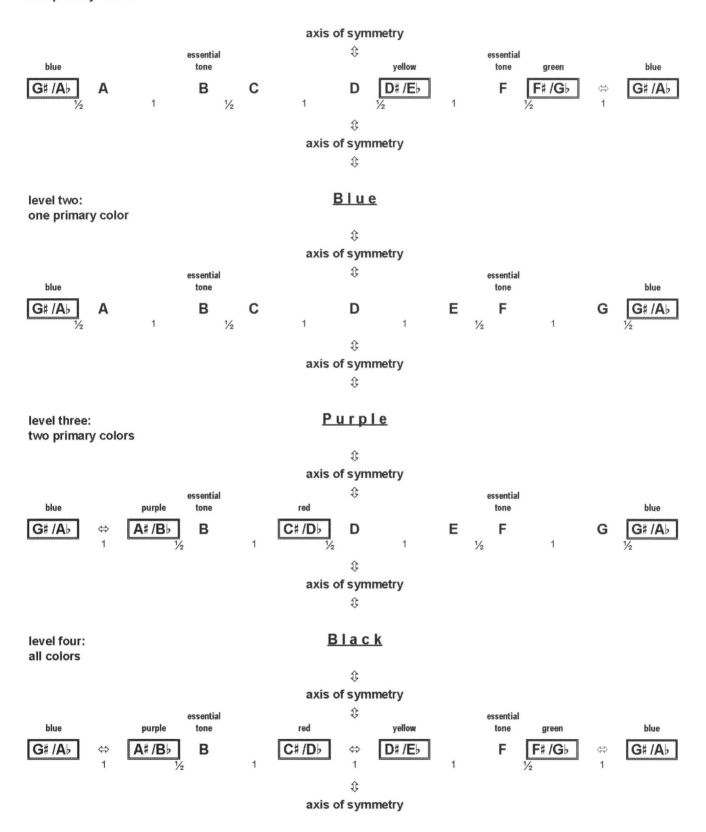

Cubic Symmetry

Shown to the right is the three-dimensional symmetry of the chromatic cube. The first level is occupied solely by the heptatonic ur-scale, shown here simply as a white corner, since it has no chromatic colorations. The mode of the ionian set represented by the white corner is determined by the composer/improviser's choice.

Any of the twelve chromatic modes may be used; however, the type of scale shown as white will always be a *major scale*. Further, the primary axis of symmetry is the second tone of the major scale, the Dorian tonic.

Level two is occupied by three scales, of which two, the red and the yellow, are ascending forms of the melodic minor scale. They are symmetrical with respect to each other and represent the most closely related minor (melodic, ascending form) modes. The third scale on level two is the eight-tone Dorian blues scale (Blue).

The third level is where the non-tonal scales reside, two octatonic diminished scales shown here as green and purple and an augmented (whole-tone) scale, shown as orange. The colors chosen reflect the primary colorations as combinations of chromatic enhancements as shown here:

- Red + Yellow = Orange
- Red + Blue = Purple
- Yellow + Blue = Green

Thus, the colors shown on level three are indicative of the sonic quality associated with the scale as a source of melodic material via the chromatic mode associated with its base white scale.

Level four is occupied by a single scale: black. It shares all colors and represents the most "outside" sounding scale choice, relative to the fundamental scale chosen within the chromatic modes. It is the major scale a tritone away from the fundamental white scale and is the farthest away from it in terms of harmonic and melodic similarity.

The primary plane of symmetry intersects the black, orange, blue and white corners.

The Chromatic Cube

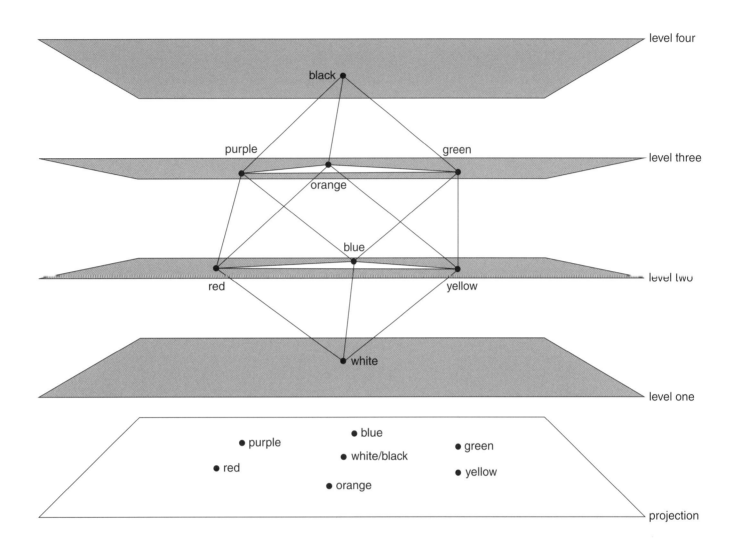

The Chromatic Molecule

Shown below is the projection of the Chromatic Cube onto a two-dimensional surface. Noteworthy is the symmetry with respect to what is now seen here as the blue-orange axis and the concept of complementary scales.

For example, the red and green scales share no common colorations, the red's C♯ (relative to C major) vs the green's E♭, F♯/G♭ and G♯/A♭.

In other words, the sound of the scales occupying opposite positions in the diagram are of a sonically contrasting nature.

The white scale is the nucleus and the others are various forms of chromatic enhancement. Further, the elevation or vertical position corresponds to the type of scale demonstrated by that particular level of chromatic enhancement:.

- Blues (octatonic Dorian blues scale and its modes)
- Diminished (whole-half and half-whole octatonic scales)
- Major scale (and its modes)
- Minor (two modes of the jazz minor scale)
- Augmented (whole-tone) scale

blue

O-- **blue**s

purple   green

O----------------------------O-------------------------- **diminished**

white / black

O-- **Major**

red   yellow

O----------------------------O-------------------------- **jazz minor**

orange

O-- **wholetone**

Chromatic Cube Scale Genres

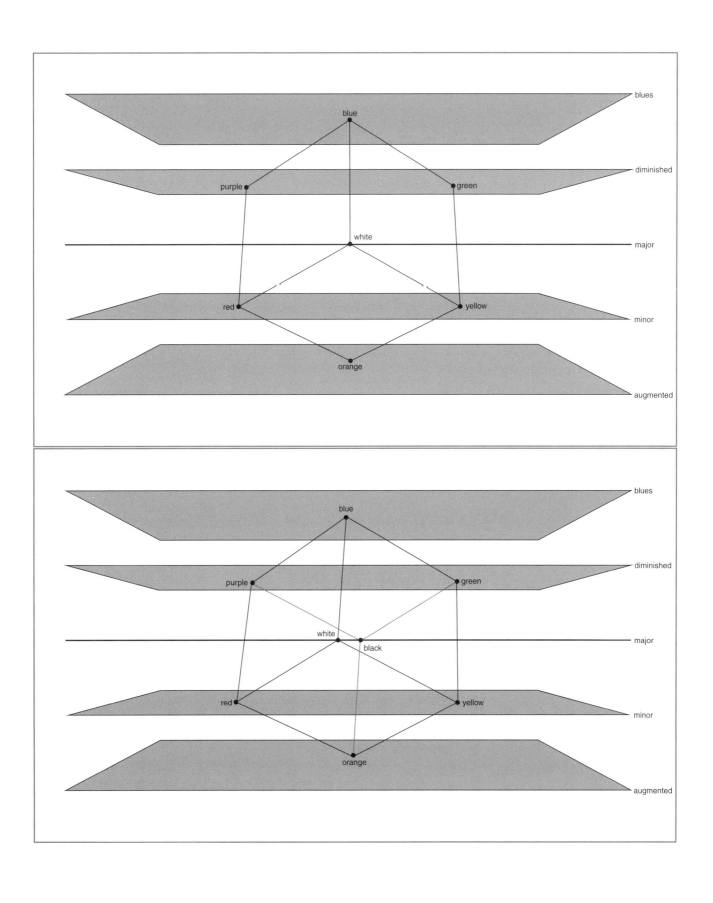

Enharmonics and the Circle of Fifths

Here are listed the twelve parent Ionian scales, along with their chromatic alterations.

The scale sets of the chromatic cube below are in the order of the Circle of Fifths:

C Major Parent

White

C	D	E	F	G	A	B

(Ionian)

Red

C♯	D	E	F	G	A	B

(jazz minor – 7th mode)

Orange

C♯	**E♭**	F	G	A	B

(whole-tone)

Yellow

C	D	**E♭**	F	G	A	B

(jazz minor)

Green

C	D	**E♭**	F	**F♯**	**G♯**	A	B

(Wh-dim)

Blue

C	D	E	F	G	**A♭**	A	B

(Bebop Major)

Purple

C♯	D	E	F	G	**G♯**	**A♯**	B

(hW-dim)

Black

D♭	E♭	F	G♭	A♭	B♭	C♭(B)

(tritone substitute of Ionian – 5th mode)

G Major Parent

White	G	A	B	C	D	E	F#	
Red	**G#**	A	B	C	D	E	F#	
Orange	**G#**	**Bb**	C	D	E	F#		
Yellow	G	A	**Bb**	C	D	E	F#	
Green	G	A	**Bb**	C	**C#**	**D#**	E	F#
Blue	G	A	B	C	D	**Eb**	E	F#
Purple	**Ab**	A	B	C	D	**Eb**	**F**	Gb
Black	Ab	Bb	C	*Db*	Eb	F	Gb	

D Major Parent

White	D	E	F#	G	A	B	C#	
Red	**D#**	E	F#	G	A	B	C#	
Orange	**D#**	**F**	G	A	B	C#		
Yellow	D	E	**F**	G	A	B	C#	
Green	D	E	**F**	G	**G#**	**A#**	B	C#
Blue	D	E	F#	G	A	**Bb**	B	C#
Purple	**Eb**	E	F#	G	A	**Bb**	**C**	Db
Black	Eb	F	G	*Ab*	Bb	C	Db	

A Major Parent

White
A   B   C#   D   E   F#   G#

Red
A#   B   C#   D   E   F#   G#

Orange
A#   **C**   D   E   F#   G#

Yellow
A   B   **C**   D   E   F#   G#

Green
A   B   **C**   D   **E**♭   **F**   G♭   A♭

Blue
A   B   C#   D   E   **F**   F#   G#

Purple
B♭   B   C#   D   E   **F**   **G**   A♭

Black
B♭   C   D   *E♭*   F   G   A♭

E Major Parent

White
E   F#   G#   A   B   C#   D#

Red
E#(**F**)   F#   G#   A   B   C#   D#

Orange
F   **G**   A   B   C#   D#

Yellow
E   F#   **G**   A   B   C#   D#

Green
E   F#   **G**   A   **B**♭   **C**   D♭   E♭

Blue
E   F#   G#   A   B   **C**   C#   D#

Purple
F   F#   G#   A   B   **C**   **D**   E♭

Black
F   G   A   *B♭*   C   D   E♭

B Major Parent

White

B	C#	D#	E	F#	G#	A#

Red

C	Db	Eb	E	Gb	Ab	Bb

Orange

C	**D**	E	Gb	Ab	Bb

Yellow

B	C#	**D**	E	F#	G#	A#

Green

B	C#	**D**	E	**F**	**G**	Ab	Bb

Blue

B	C#	D#	E	F#	**G**	G#	A#

Purple

C	C#	D#	E	F#	**G**	**A**	Bb

Black

C	D	E	*F*	G	A	Bb

F♯/G♭ Major Parent

White

Gb	Ab	Bb	Cb(B)	Db	Eb	F

Red

G	Ab	Bb	Cb(B)	Db	Eb	F

Orange

G	**A**	B	Db	Eb	F

Yellow

F#	G#	**A**	B	C#	D#	E#(F)

Green

F#	G#	**A**	B	**C**	**D**	Eb	F

Blue

Gb	Ab	Bb	Cb(B)	Db	**D**	Eb	F

Purple

G	G#	A#	B	C#	**D**	**E**	F

Black

G	A	B	*C*	D	E	F

D♭ Major Parent

White
D♭ E♭ F G♭ A♭ B♭ C

Red
D E♭ F G♭ A♭ B♭ C

Orange
D **E** G♭ A♭ B♭ C

Yellow
D♭ E♭ **F♭(E)** G♭ A♭ B♭ C

Green
C♯ D♯ **E** F♯ **G** **A** B♭ C

Blue
D♭ E♭ F G♭ A♭ **A** B♭ C

Purple
D E♭ F G♭ A♭ **A** **B** C

Black
D E F♯ *G* A B C

A♭ Major Parent

White
A♭ B♭ C D♭ E♭ F G

Red
A B♭ C D♭ E♭ F G

Orange
A **B** D♭ E♭ F G

Yellow
A♭ B♭ **C♭(B)** D♭ E♭ F G

Green
G♯ A♯ **B** C♯ **D** **E** F G

Blue
A♭ B♭ C D♭ E♭ **E** F G

Purple
A B♭ C D♭ E♭ **E** **F♯** G

Black
A B C♯ *D* E F♯ G

E♭ Major Parent

White
E♭ F G A♭ B♭ C D

Red
E F G A♭ B♭ C D

Orange
E **G♭** A♭ B♭ C D

Yellow
E♭ F **G♭** A♭ B♭ C D

Green
E♭ F **G♭** A♭ **A** **B** C D

Blue
E♭ F G A♭ B♭ **B** C D

Purple
E F G A♭ B♭ **B** **C♯** D

Black
E F♯ G♯ *A* B C♯ D

B♭ Major Parent

White
B♭ C D E♭ F G A

Red
B C D E♭ F G A

Orange
B **D♭** E♭ F G A

Yellow
B♭ C **D♭** E♭ F G A

Green
B♭ C **D♭** E♭ **E** **F♯** G A

Blue
B♭ C D E♭ F **G♭** G A

Purple
B C D E♭ F **F♯** **G♯** A

Black
B C♯ D♯ *E* F♯ G♯ A

F Major Parent

White
| F | G | A | B♭ | C | D | E |

Red
| **F♯** | G | A | B♭ | C | D | E |

Orange
| **G♭** | **A♭** | B♭ | C | D | E |

Yellow
| F | G | **A♭** | B♭ | C | D | E |

Green
| F | G | **A♭** | B♭ | **B** | **C♯** | D | E |

Blue
| F | G | A | B♭ | C | **C♯** | D | E |

Purple
| **F♯** | G | A | B♭ | C | **C♯** | **D♯** | E |

Black
| F♯ | G♯ | A♯ | *B* | C♯ | D♯ | E |

This is a chromatic system, with the intention of giving the composer/improviser free and uninhibited access to the entire chromatic scale.

The white notes consist of the *first* seven letters of the alphabet, in atonal situations, a convenient way to label the five black notes is with the *last* five letters of the alphabet:

$$\mathbf{V} = C\sharp/D\flat$$

$$\mathbf{W} = D\sharp/E\flat$$

$$\mathbf{X} = F\sharp/G\flat$$

$$\mathbf{Y} = G\sharp/A\flat$$

$$\mathbf{Z} = A\sharp/B\flat$$

This also works well in solfeggio as each of those letters can be sung as one syllable (*vee, dub, ex, why, zed*).

C Major Parent

White	C	D	E	F	G	A	B
Red	**V**	D	E	F	G	A	B
Orange	**V**	**W**	F	G	A	B	
Yellow	C	D	**W**	F	G	A	B
Green	C	D	**W**	F	**X**	**Y**	A	B
Blue	C	D	E	F	G	**Y**	A	B
Purple	**V**	D	E	F	G	**Y**	**Z**	B
Black	**V**	**W**	F	*X*	**Y**	**Z**	B

G Major Parent

White	G	A	B	C	D	E	**X**
Red	**Y**	A	B	C	D	E	**X**
Orange	**Y**	**Z**	C	D	E	**X**	
Yellow	G	A	**Z**	C	D	E	**X**
Green	G	A	**Z**	C	**V**	**W**	E	**X**
Blue	G	A	B	C	D	**W**	E	**X**
Purple	**Y**	A	B	C	D	**W**	F	**X**
Black	**Y**	**Z**	C	*V*	**W**	F	**X**

D Major Parent

White
D	E	**X**	G	A	B	**V**	

Red
W	E	**X**	G	A	B	**V**	

Orange
W	F	G	A	B	**V**	

Yellow
D	E	F	G	A	B	**V**	

Green
D	E	F	G	**Y**	**Z**	B	**V**

Blue
D	E	**X**	G	A	**Z**	B	**V**

Purple
W	E	**X**	G	A	**Z**	C	**V**

Black
W	F	G	*Y*	**Z**	C	**V**	

A Major Parent

White
A	B	**V**	D	E	**X**	**Y**	

Red
Z	B	**V**	D	E	**X**	**Y**	

Orange
Z	C	D	E	**X**	**Y**	

Yellow
A	B	C	D	E	**X**	**Y**	

Green
A	B	C	D	**W**	F	**X**	**Y**

Blue
A	B	**V**	D	E	F	**X**	**Y**

Purple
Z	B	**V**	D	E	F	G	**Y**

Black
Z	C	D	*W*	F	G	**Y**	

E Major Parent

White
E	**X**	**Y**	A	B	**V**	**W**

Red
F	**X**	**Y**	A	B	**V**	**W**

Orange
F	G	A	B	**V**	**W**

Yellow
E	**X**	G	A	B	**V**	**W**

Green
E	**X**	G	A	**Z**	C	**V**	**W**

Blue
E	**X**	**Y**	A	B	C	**V**	**W**

Purple
F	**X**	**Y**	A	B	C	D	**W**

Black
F	G	A	**Z**	C	D	**W**

B Major Parent

White
B	**V**	**W**	E	**X**	**Y**	**Z**

Red
C	**V**	**W**	E	**X**	**Y**	**Z**

Orange
C	D	E	**X**	**Y**	**Z**

Yellow
B	**V**	D	E	**X**	**Y**	**Z**

Green
B	**V**	D	E	F	G	**Y**	**Z**

Blue
B	**V**	**W**	E	**X**	G	**Y**	**Z**

Purple
C	**V**	**W**	E	**X**	G	A	**Z**

Black
C	D	E	*F*	G	A	**Z**

G♭ Major Parent

White
X   **Y**   **Z**   B   **V**   **W**   F

Red
G   **Y**   **Z**   B   **V**   **W**   F

Orange
G   A   B   **V**   **W**   F

Yellow
X   **Y**   A   B   **V**   **W**   F

Green
X   **Y**   A   B   C   D   **W**   F

Blue
X   **Y**   **Z**   B   **V**   D   **W**   F

Purple
G   **Y**   **Z**   B   **V**   D   E   F

Black
G   A   B   *C*   D   E   F

D♭ Major Parent

White
V   **W**   F   **X**   **Y**   **Z**   C

Red
D   **W**   F   **X**   **Y**   **Z**   C

Orange
D   E   **X**   **Y**   **Z**   C

Yellow
V   **W**   E   **X**   **Y**   **Z**   C

Green
V   **W**   E   **X**   G   A   **Z**   C

Blue
V   **W**   F   **X**   **Y**   A   **Z**   C

Purple
D   **W**   F   **X**   **Y**   A   B   C

Black
D   E   **X**   *G*   A   B   C

A♭ Major Parent

White
Y   **Z**   C   **V**   **W**   F   G

Red
A   **Z**   C   **V**   **W**   F   G

Orange
A   B   **V**   **W**   F   G

Yellow
Y   **Z**   B   **V**   **W**   F   G

Green
Y   **Z**   B   **V**   D   E   F   G

Blue
Y   **Z**   C   **V**   **W**   E   F   G

Purple
A   **Z**   C   **V**   **W**   E   **X**   G

Black
A   B   **V**   *D*   E   **X**   G

E♭ Major Parent

White
W   F   G   **Y**   **Z**   C   D

Red
E   F   G   **Y**   **Z**   C   D

Orange
E   **X**   **Y**   **Z**   C   D

Yellow
W   F   **X**   **Y**   **Z**   C   D

Green
W   F   **X**   **Y**   A   B   C   D

Blue
W   F   G   **Y**   **Z**   B   C   D

Purple
E   F   G   **Y**   **Z**   B   **V**   D

Black
E   **X**   **Y**   *A*   B   **V**   D

B♭ Major Parent

White
Z	C	D	**W**	F	G	A

Red
B	C	D	**W**	F	G	A

Orange
B	**V**	**W**	F	G	A

Yellow
Z	C	**V**	**W**	F	G	A

Green
Z	C	**V**	**W**	E	**X**	G	A

Blue
Z	C	D	**W**	F	**X**	G	A

Purple
B	C	D	**W**	F	**X**	**Y**	A

Black
B	**V**	**W**	*E*	**X**	**Y**	A

F Major Parent

White
F	G	A	**Z**	C	D	E

Red
X	G	A	**Z**	C	D	E

Orange
X	**Y**	**Z**	C	D	E

Yellow
F	G	**Y**	**Z**	C	D	E

Green
F	G	**Y**	**Z**	B	**V**	D	E

Blue
F	G	A	**Z**	C	**V**	D	E

Purple
X	G	A	**Z**	C	**V**	**W**	E

Black
X	**Y**	**Z**	*B*	**V**	**W**	E

This completes the list of scales defined by the chromatic cube, a graphic representation of the scale choices for use in melody and harmony.

The real benefit of all this is that once a parent scale is chosen, the chromatic realm is opened up through the relational characteristics of the different scale types.

The colors actually describe, with familiar ease, how the listener may perceive the melody through the scales. For example, blue and red make purple and in this case, the primary colors red and blue represent tones from their respective scales. Both red and blue tones are found in the purple scale, and the purple scale shares properties of both scales from which its components (red and blue) are derived.

The chromatic cube is a simple visualization including all tones from the chromatic scale, which is shown as a radially symmetric expansion of the parent ionian scale.

Following are examples of other types of symmetry within the chromatic cube. Take a look at the following tetrahedronal split complementary relationships, which describe scales not directly related to each other.

Complementary Tetrahedrons

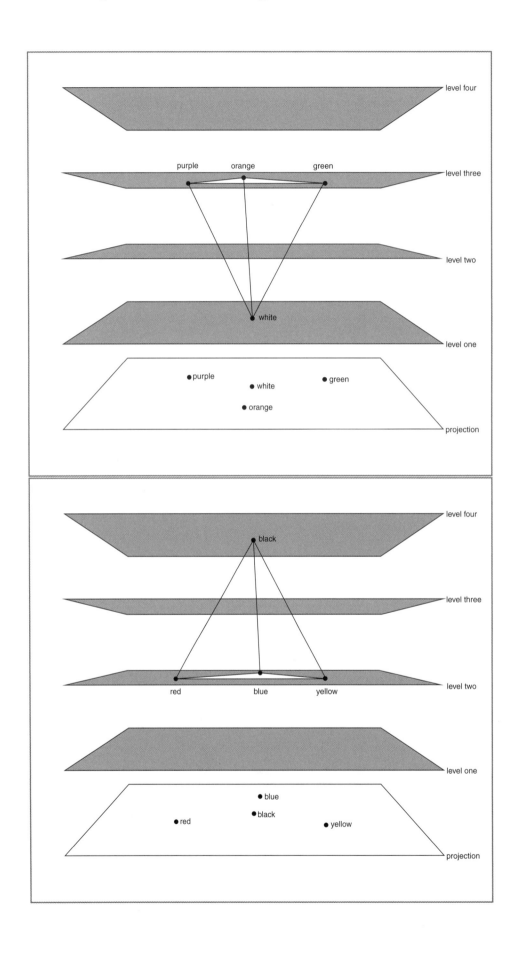

Other Forms of Symmetry

Since scales (and their constituent tones) and relationships between them have been shown as a graphic representation of a familiar three-dimensional object, the cube, it is now a simple matter to describe other forms of symmetry between them. For example, diagramming the relationships between the various scales, two tetrahedrons may be generated which would show a "split complementary" pattern like this:

2 tetrahedrons

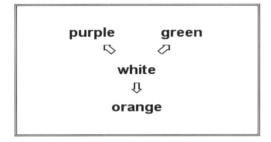 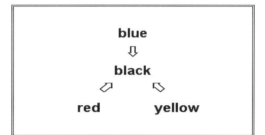

The diagrams opposite this page may be used to help show the inherent properties of a set of eight objects displaying a cubic symmetry. There are three basic relational characteristics:

1) Adjacent (linear [edges] - most closely related)

2) Split complementary (tetrahedronal [neither adjacent nor opposite])

3) Complementary (opposite, most distant)

To demonstrate the concept of opposites, here is an example to showing complementary relationships:

Over a Gm7 C7 (parent = F major) vamp play

1) F major in contrast to B major [white vs black]

[F G A B♭ C D E]   [F♯ G♯ A♯ B C♯ D♯ E]

2) G melodic minor in contrast to F Wh-diminished [red vs green]

[F♯ G A B♭ C D E]   [F G A♭ B♭ B C♯ D E]

3) F melodic minor in contrast to G Wh-diminished [yellow vs purple]

[F G A♭ B♭ C D E]   [F♯ G A B♭ C C♯ D♯ E]

4) G♭ whole-tone in contrast to G eight-tone blues [orange vs blue]

[G♭ A♭ B♭ C D E]   [F G A B♭ C D♭ D E]

and observe the differences in sound. Since all of the scales have the essential tones B♭ and E, there is a sonic similarity in all of these scales; however, the differences between them are striking.

Chromatic Cube Analyses

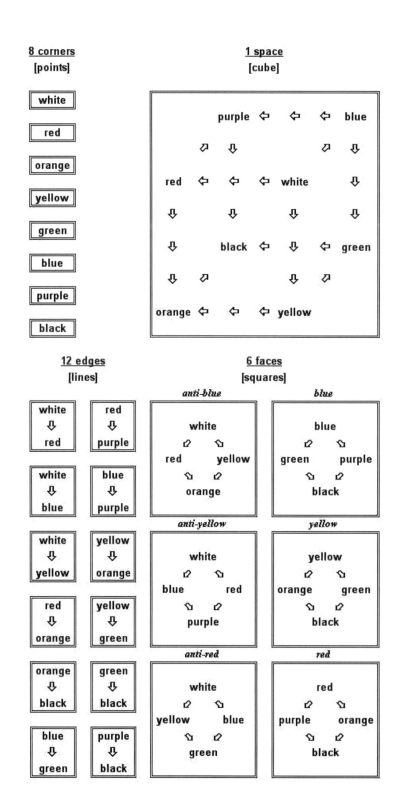

8 corners
[points]

- white
- red
- orange
- yellow
- green
- blue
- purple
- black

1 space
[cube]

purple ⇦ ⇦ ⇦ blue

red ⇦ ⇦ ⇦ white

black ⇦ ⇦ green

orange ⇦ ⇦ ⇦ yellow

12 edges
[lines]

white ⇩ red

white ⇩ blue

white ⇩ yellow

red ⇩ orange

orange ⇩ black

blue ⇩ green

red ⇩ purple

blue ⇩ purple

yellow ⇩ orange

yellow ⇩ green

green ⇩ black

purple ⇩ black

6 faces
[squares]

anti-blue

white

red yellow

orange

blue

blue

green purple

black

anti-yellow

white

blue red

purple

yellow

yellow

orange green

black

anti-red

white

yellow blue

green

red

red

purple orange

black

Octahedronal Symmetry

The faces of a cube exhibit an octahedronal* symmetry in that the six faces may be used to group the corners (scales) into certain types of families:

Red family: all scales containing a red component
Red, orange, purple, and black

Anti-red family: all scales missing a red component
White, yellow, blue, and green

Yellow family: all scales containing a yellow component
Yellow, orange, green, and black

Anti-yellow family: all scales missing a yellow component
White, red, blue, and purple

Blue family: all scales containing a blue component
Green, blue, purple, and black

Anti-blue family: all scales missing a blue component
White, red, yellow, and orange

(See also page 219)

* An octahedron is an eight-sided object with six vertices, each of which may represent the center of a side of a cube...

Octahedron

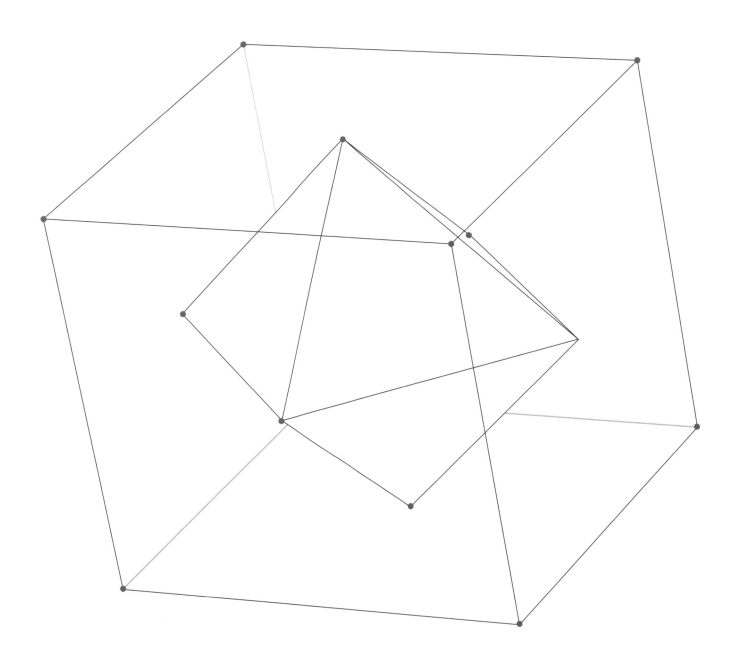

Chromatic Cube Accidental Conventions

For seven note diatonic scales, each component receives a different letter.

Applying the red alteration to the parent Ionian raises the **1**:

$$\sharp\underline{\mathbf{1}}\ 2\ 3\ 4\ 5\ 6\ 7$$
(Jazz Minor - 7th mode)

Applying the yellow alteration to the parent lowers the **3rd**:

$$1\ 2\ \flat\underline{\mathbf{3}}\ 4\ 5\ 6\ 7$$
(Jazz Minor)

Applying the orange raises the **1**, lowers the **3rd**, and squeezes out the **2nd**:

$$\sharp\underline{\mathbf{1}}\ \flat\underline{\mathbf{3}}\ 4\ 5\ 6\ 7$$
(Whole-Tone)

The blue is not an alteration. It is an addition to the parent:

$$1\ 2\ 3\ 4\ 5\ \sharp\underline{\mathbf{5}}/\flat\underline{\mathbf{6}}\ 6\ 7$$
(Bebop Major)

In the case of the diminished modes, one of the letters must be doubled. The decision of naming each accidental is determined by the identities of the minor tetrachords which make up the scale.

ex: B Wh-dim scale = [B minor tetrachord] h [F minor tetrachord]

[B C♯ D E] h [F G A♭ B♭]

The green lowers the **3rd**, raises the **5th**, and adds in a ♯**4**:

$$1\ 2\ \flat\underline{\mathbf{3}}\ 4\ \sharp\underline{\mathbf{4}}\ \sharp\underline{\mathbf{5}}\ 6\ 7$$
(Wh-dim)

Purple raises the **1**, lowers the **6th**, and adds in a ♭**7**:

$$\sharp\underline{\mathbf{1}}\ 2\ 3\ 4\ 5\ \flat\underline{\mathbf{6}}\ \flat\underline{\mathbf{7}}\ 7$$
(hW-dim)

Black is expressed as its most typical Ionian spelling.

The Harmonic Series and the Search for Perfect Chords

The Harmonic Series lays the foundation for the establishment of fixed frequencies for musical pitches. Shown here are the first six notes in the harmonic series from the starting note C:

1	2	3	4	5	6
C	C	G	C	E	G

The Arabic numerals above represent whole number multiples of the fundamental frequency (the first harmonic) and can be demonstrated by playing harmonics on any stringed instrument or by over-blowing wind and brass instruments.

Intervals are defined by the distance between them. For example, to hear the exact interval between the second harmonic and third harmonic (a perfect fifth), play the twelfth fret harmonic on any guitar string followed by the seventh fret harmonic.

The Major and Minor Triads are unique in that they are the only two triads consisting solely of *consonant* intervals:

Minor Third, *ideal frequency ratio 6/5*

Major Third, *ideal frequency ratio 5/4*

Perfect Fourth, *ideal frequency ratio 4/3*

Perfect Fifth, *ideal frequency ratio 3/2*

Minor Sixth, *ideal frequency ratio 8/5*

Major Sixth, *ideal frequency ratio 5/3*

There also exists the perfect unison, *ideal frequency ratio 1/1*, and the perfect octave, *ideal frequency ratio 2/1*.

(Twelve-tone equal tempered frequency ratios are slightly altered in order to preserve consistency in key modulations, but a discussion of that is beyond the scope of this book.)

The table below shows the relationships of the intervals within the major and minor triads:

Major Triad (close position)		Minor Triad (close position)	
G	Fifth	G	Fifth
	} Minor Third		} Major Third
E	Third	E♭	Third
	} Major Third		} Minor Third
C	Root	C	Root

The stacking of alternating major and minor thirds, producing perfect fifths, is the cornerstone of the perfect chord types. The perfect fifth intervals between the roots and fifths, thirds and sevenths, fifths and ninths, sevenths and elevenths, and finally between the ninths and thirteenths are what makes them "perfect" for use in outlining many chord types.

Organizing pitches by an alternating m3-M3-m3 interval pattern with the central axis of symmetry located at D yields the following "octatonic" radially symmetrical chord:

Dm13 - F13♯11

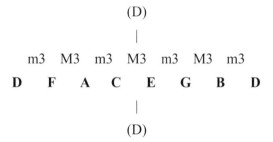

```
                        (D)
                         |
           m3  M3  m3  M3  m3  M3  m3
         D   F   A   C   E   G   B   D
                         |
                        (D)
```

Note that not only is D the central point, it is also both the top and bottom note in this set.

B	13		D	13	
		} Major Third			} Minor Third
G	11		B	♯11	
		} Minor Third			} Major Third
E	9		G	9	
		} Major Third			} Minor Third
C	♭7		E	7	
		} Minor Third			} Major Third
A	5		C	5	
		} Major Third			} Minor Third
F	♭3		A	3	
		} Minor Third			} Major Third
D	1		F	1	

When laid out in a stepwise order (rather than arpeggiated as shown above) two scales may be derived:

1) Dorian

| 1 | 2 | ♭3 | 4 | 5 | 6 | ♭7 |

2) Lydian

| 1 | 2 | 3 | ♯4 | 5 | 6 | 7 |

These are the scales implied by a "type 1 perfect minor chord" (m13) and a "type 1 perfect major chord" (maj13♯11) and their inversions/voicings.

These represent the "type 1 perfect minor and major heptatonic scales". It is possible to use them as melodic material over many chords, in isolation, without regard to either the previous or subsequent chord, ie. without any harmonic and/or temporal context.

This type of perfect chord used in its entirety in root position works over Dm (acting as either a ii chord or sometimes as a i chord) and F major (acting as either a IV chord or sometimes as a I chord).

This pitch set (and its subsets) can work over the following 48 common and useful chords:

Dm, D2, D4, Dm6, Dm7, Dm7sus4, Dm69, Dm9, Dm11, Dm13

F, F2, F6, Fmaj7, F69, Fmaj9, Fmaj9♯11, Fmaj13♯11

Am, A2, A4, Am7, Am7sus4, Am9, Am11

C, C2, C4, C6, Cmaj7, C69, Cmaj9, Cmaj13

Em, E4, Em7, Em7sus4

G, G2, G4, G6, G7, G7sus4, G69, G9, G11, G13

Bm7♭5

(For inversions of type 1 perfect chords, see appendix pages 140-141).

Radial Symmetry Type 2

In this second type of radial symmetry, the primary axis falls squarely between two adjacent half-steps.

For the examples here, our central point is between the notes E and F

(E½♯ - F½♭)

Radial Symmetry Type 2:
Scales

C Bebop Dominant Scale

B C D E F G A B♭

h W W h W W h

B Wh-Diminished Scale

B C♯ D E F G A♭ B♭

W h W h W h W

C♯ Major Blues Scale

B C♯ E F G♯ A♯

W m3 h m3 W

C♯ Open Harmonic Scale (no 3rd)

B♯ C♯ D♯ F♯ G♯ A

h W m3 W h

G Open Harmonic Scale (no 3rd)

C D E♭ F♯ G A

W h m3 h W

B Major 13th (no 11th)

B C♯ D♯ F♯ G♯ A♯

W W m3 W W

Radial Symmetry Type 2:
Chords

Dm11 (no 7th)

D   EF   G

W   h   W

D♭ (add b3)

D♭   EF   A♭

m3   h   m3

Fmaj7 (2nd inversion)

C   EF   A

M3   h   M3

Db24 (D♭ double-sus)

D♭   E♭   G♭   A♭

W   m3   W

C diminished 7th

C   E♭   G♭   A

m3   m3   m3

Bmaj7

B   D♯   F♯   A♯

M3   m3   M3

G♯m11

G♯   B   D♯   F♯   A♯   C♯

m3   M3   m3   M3   m3

G24 (G double-sus)

C   D   G   A

W   P4   W

Perfect Chords Type 2

Choosing the axis of symmetry to be the mid-point between F and F♯ (the 11th harmonic of C), then applying and expanding the repeating radial symmetry type two pattern "M3-m3-M3" yields the following hexad:

Am11 - Cmaj13(no 11)

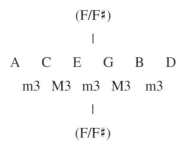

This is the "perfect chord type 2". It works perfectly in its entirety in root position over both Am (acting as either a **vi chord**, a **i chord**, or as a **ii chord**) and C major (acting as either a **I chord** or as a **IV chord**).

By not including an F or an F♯, the level of ambiguity is increased and therefore it can *always* be used in its entirety in more root position situations than "perfect chord type 1".

In addition, its lack of a tritone (F-B or F♯-C) means no tension / tendencies whatsoever, resulting in perfect consonance for both the A minor and C major quality chords.

Consequently, these chords really can "stand alone" without any harmonic and/or temporal context.

This radially symmetrical hexatonic pitch set (or its subsets) may be also used over the following 41 common and useful chords:

F (rootless), F2, F6, Fmaj7, F69, Fmaj9, Fmaj9♯11, Fmaj13♯11

Am, A2, A4, Am7, Am7sus4, Am9, Am11

C, C2, C6, Cmaj7, C69, Cmaj9, Cmaj13(no11)

Em, E4, Em7, Em7sus4

G, G2, G4, G6, G69

Bm7(no 5)

D5, D2, D4, D(open)6, D(open)7, D7sus4, D(open)9, D9sus4, D(open)69

NB: The pitch set A C E G B D rearranged stepwise is G A B C D E (ut/do re mi fa sol la) and is identical to Guido's base hexatonic gamut.

An interesting thing happens when this same radial symmetry type 2 pattern is expanded out to the next level:

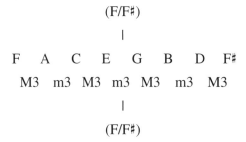

Note that the axis of symmetry for this octatonic pitch set is F/F#, and that an F is introduced at the bottom and an F# is introduced at the top.

This octatonic pitch set (or its subsets) may be used with the following 72 common and useful chords:

F, F2, F6, Fmaj7, F69, Fmaj9, Fmaj9#11, Fmaj13#11

Am, A2, A4, Am6, Am7, Am7sus4, Am69, Am9, Am11, Am13

C, C2, C4, C6, Cmaj7, C69, Cmaj9, Cmaj9#11, Cmaj13, Cmaj13#11

Em, E2, E4, Em7, Em7sus4, Em9, Em11

G, G2, G4, G7, G7sus4, G9, G13

G6, Gmaj7, G69, Gmaj9, Gmaj13

Dm, D2, D4, Dm6, Dm7, Dm7sus4, Dm69, Dm9, Dm11, Dm13

D, D6, D7, D7sus4, D7#9, D9, D69, D9sus4, D11, D13

Bm, Bm7, Bm7sus4, Bm7♭5

F#m7♭5

The octatonic scales derived from this radial symmetry type 2 pattern
(M3-m3-M3-m3-M3-m3-M3) are identical to
the G bebop dominant scale (G A B C D E F F# G) and its modes.

For more information on octatonic scales which are formed by the addition of an accidental to common heptatonic scales, see appendices pages 192-199.

Appendices

Circle of Fourths

C

G

F

D

B♭

A

E♭

E

A♭

B

D♭

G♭

Altered 7th Chords

The notes most likely to be altered are the 9ths and the 5ths.

When playing a 7alt chord, the defining tones of the chord (3rd & ♭7) are not the object of any alterations.

A natural 4th (11th) note is not considered "altered" because
it's the natural extension of tertian harmony.

The ♯11 (♯4) note is the same as a ♭5. In general, "the 4th (11th)" is not altered in a 7alt chord (although the notations 7♯4 and 7♯11 are frequently found).

Lowering the thirteenth is equal to sharping the five.
(Flat 13th also shows up in charts from time to time.)

With the 9th you have two possible alterations: sharp and flat (♯ & ♭).
Same with the 5th: diminished & augmented.

That yields four basic possible combinations:

7♭5♯9

7♭5♭9

7♯5♯9

7♯5♭9

There doesn't necessarily need to be a "minimum" of 2 alterations. Often one alteration is enough. This yields another 4 choices:

7♯5

7♭5

7♯9

7♭9

If we choose to alter the tonic note, its substitute is the ♯IV.

With pianists, the rootless chord crowd uses two voicings as a typical LH accompaniment when encountering a "7alt" chord in a chart:

7♯5♯9 chord
voiced as:
7 ♯9 3 ♯5
or
3 ♯5 7 ♯9.

Notice that the above jazz piano voicings are the standard rootless ones for the tritone substitute dominant 13th (no 11) chord.

For those unfamiliar with the Evans' rootless system, here's an example of this variation of G7alt:

G7♯5♯9 = F [♭7th]   A♯/B♭ [♯9th]   B/C♭ [3rd]   D♯/E♭ [♯5th]

An analysis of G7's tritone substitute [D♭7] yields
(using the same exact notes):

D♭13 = F [3rd]   B♭/A♯ [6th/13th]   C♭/B [♭7th]   E♭/D♯ [9th]

This implies that it might be a reasonable strategy (if you have to "think fast" in a live situation) to use the typical rootless tritone substitute when encountering the "7alt" indication.

Examples:
D♭7 analyzed as G7alt = D♭ [♭5th] - F [♭7th] - A♭ [♭9th] - B/C♭ [3rd]
D♭9 analyzed as G7alt = as above, but add D♯/E♭ [♯5th]

This is not the only strategy and perhaps not even the best, but it certainly should be taken into consideration as a serious contender when searching for the "ideal voicing" for an alt7 chord.

There are instances where both a ♭9 AND ♯9 are used simultaneously to great effect. This yields a few other interesting possibilities:

7♭9♯9

7♭5♭9♯9

7♯5♭9♯9

The same holds true for double-altered 5ths:

7♭5♯5

7♭5♯5♭9

7♭5♯5♯9

Use of WholeTone scales over alt7 chords

The whole tone scale is often chosen over both 7♭5 & 7♯5 chords. Omitting the most offensive tone leaves you with a "Lydian" (whole tone scale) style pentatonic mode.

Use of Diminished scales over alt7 chords

Over a 7♭9 you can use the dim(h-W) scale.

For C7alt that would be | C - D♭ - D♯ - E - F♯ - G - A - B♭ - C |

Each chord tone in this case (except the root) has an accompanying note a half-step below it acting as its leading tone.

D♯ -> E

F♯ -> G

A -> B♭

Use of Phrygian dominant scale over 7♭9 chords

Over a 7♭9 you can also use the Phrygian dominant scale.

For C7♭9 that would be | C - D♭ - E - F - G - A♭ - B♭ - C |

Use of Jazz Minor Modes over alt7 chords

Construction of the "dim-WT" scale (diminished-whole tone) with C as its root:

The first four notes are the diminished tetrachord:

[h W h = C - D♭ - E♭ - F♭]

The second four notes are the Lydian tetrachord:

[partial Whole Tone scale = W W W = G♭ - A♭ - B♭ - C]

Also note that the jazz altered scale (aka "diminished-wholetone scale", "altered dominant scale", "Superlocrian scale") is the 7th mode of the Jazz Minor scale.

The altered dominant scale is a good candidate for soloing over many altered dominant chords. It contains all of the possible alterations (♭9 ♯9 ♭5 ♯5), and ALL of the defining chord tones (1 3 ♭7) too.

This scale analyzed over a C7alt chord would be:

C	D♭	D♯	E	G♭	G♯	B♭	C
root	[♭9th]	[♯9th]	[3rd]	[♭5th]	[♯5th]	[♭7th]	root

If we were to use a ♯IV7 substitute (F♯7) for our C7alt chord,
using the exactly same notes yields the
"F♯ Lydian dominant scale"
(4th mode of the jazz minor scale):

C/B♯	D♭/C♯	D♯	E	G♭/F♯	G♯	B♭/A♯	C/B♯
[♯4th/♯11th]	[5th]	[6th/13th]	[♭7th]	root	[2nd/9th]	[3rd]	[♯4th/♯11th]

F♯	G♯	A♯	B♯	C♯	D♯	E	F♯
root	[2nd/9th]	[3rd]	[♯4th/♯11th]	[5th]	[6th/13th]	[♭7th]	root

If there happens to be a note in there that you like less than others,
don't play it so much.

When searching for the perfect alt7 chord, always look to the music itself. Do what the changes and current tonal center suggest to your ear.

Tetrachord Combos

	[G dim] Bb ⇩	[G lyd] A ⇩	[G dim] Ab ⇩	[G dim][G lyd] G ⇩
[Db dim] E ⇨	(#9) (13) **G7** (13) (#9) **Db 7**	(9) (13) **G7** (#5) (#9) **Db 7**	(b9) (13) **G7** (5) (#9) **Db 7**	(8) (13) **G7** (b5) (#9) **Db 7**
[Db lyd] Eb ⇨	(#9) (#5) **G7** (13) (9) **Db 7**	(9) (#5) **G7** (#5) (9) **Db 7**	(b9) (#5) **G7** (5) (9) **Db 7**	(8) (#5) **G7** (b5) (9) **Db 7**
[Db dim] D ⇨	(#9) (5) **G7** (13) (b9) **Db 7**	(9) (5) **G7** (#5) (b9) **Db 7**	(b9) (5) **G7** (5) (b9) **Db 7**	(8) (5) **G7** (b5) (b9) **Db 7**
[Db dim][Db lyd] Db ⇨	(#9) (b5) **G7** (13) (8) **Db 7**	(9) (b5) **G7** (#5) (8) **Db 7**	(b9) (b5) **G7** (5) (8) **Db 7**	(8) (b5) **G7** (b5) (8) **Db 7**

Analysis of Combinations of Diminished Tetrachords and Lydian Tetrachords and Their Use with Altered Dominant Chords

The "G diminished tetrachord"

[G dTC]

G   A♭   B♭   B

The G Lydian (whole-tone) tetrachord

[G LTC]

G   A   B   D♭

The D♭ diminished tetrachord

[D♭ dTC]

D♭   D   E   F

The D♭ Lydian (whole-tone) tetrachord

[D♭ LTC]

D♭   E♭   F   G

The number between the brackets indicates

the number of half-steps separating the tetrachords, examples:

["tetrachord"] 0 ["tetrachord"] = overlapping/no separation (bold/underlined)

["tetrachord"] 1 ["tetrachord"] = one half-step separation (divided by |)

["tetrachord"] 2 ["tetrachord"] = a whole-step separation (divided by ||)

[G LTC] 0 [D♭ dTC]

G   A   B   **D♭**   D   E   F

G lydian dominant scale

the same pitch set as

[D♭ dTC] 2 [G LTC]

D♭   D   E   F   ‖   G   A   B   D♭

D♭ jazz altered scale

(aka Superlocrian mode, dim-WT scale, etc)

[G dTC] 2 [D♭ LTC]

G   A♭   B♭   B ‖ D♭   E♭   F   G

G jazz altered scale

(aka Superlocrian mode, dim-WT scale, etc)

the same pitch set as

[D♭ LTC] 0 [G dTC]

D♭   E♭   F   **G**   A♭   B♭   B

D♭ Lydian dominant scale

* * *

[G dTC] 2 [D♭ dTC]

G   A♭   B♭   B ‖ D♭   D   E   F

G half-whole diminished scale

the same pitch set as

[D♭ dTC] 2 [G dTC]

D♭   D   E   F ‖ G   A♭   B♭   B

D♭ half-whole diminished scale

* * *

[G LTC] 0 [D♭ LTC]

G   A   B   **D♭**   E♭   F   G

G whole-tone scale

the same pitch set as

[D♭ LTC] 0 [G LTC]

D♭   E♭   F   **G**   A   B   D♭

D♭ whole-tone scale

* * *

Simple voicings containing only the thirds and ♭7ths of the chords G7 and D♭7 may be embellished with any of the above scales or pitch sets, as both the thirds and ♭7ths are common to all of the above scales:

B F   F B

Part One: Three-Note Voicings

Adding extensions and/or alterations to
these basic 3rd and ♭7th three-note voicings,
the following scales will fit:

♭5	D♭	1
3	B	♭7
♭7	F	3
G7♭5		**D♭7**

G Lydian dominant
[G LTC] 0 [D♭ dTC]

D♭ jazz altered
[D♭ dTC] 2 [G LTC]

G jazz altered
[G dTC] 2 [D♭ LTC]

D♭ Lydian dominant
[D♭ LTC] 0 [G dTC]

G half-whole diminished
[G dTC] 2 [Db dTC]

D♭ half-whole diminished
[D♭ dTC] 2 [G dTC]

G whole-tone
[G LTC] 0 [D♭ LTC]

D♭ whole-tone
[D♭ LTC] 0 [G LTC]

5	D	♭9
3	B	♭7
♭7	F	3
G7		**D♭7♭9**

G Lydian dominant
[G LTC] 0 [D♭ dTC]

D♭ jazz altered
[D♭ dTC] 2 [G LTC]

G half-whole diminished
[G dTC] 2 [D♭ dTC]

D♭ half-whole diminished
[D♭ dTC] 2 [G dTC]

#5	E♭	9
3	B	♭7
♭7	F	3
G7#5		**D♭9**

G jazz altered
[G dTC] 2 [D♭ LTC]

D♭ Lydian dominant
[D♭ LTC] 0 [G dTC]

G whole-tone
[G LTC] 0 [D♭ LTC]

D♭ whole-tone
[D♭ LTC] 0 [G LTC]

13	E	♯9
3	B	♭7
♭7	F	3
G13		**D♭7♯9**

G Lydian dominant

[G LTC] 0 [D♭ dTC]

D♭ jazz altered

[D♭ dTC] 2 [G LTC]

G half-whole diminished

[G dTC] 2 [D♭ dTC]

D♭ half-whole diminished

[D♭ dTC] 2 [G dTC]

1	G	♭5
♭7	F	3
3	B	♭7
G7		**D♭7♭5**

G Lydian dominant

[G LTC] 0 [D♭ dTC]

D♭ jazz altered

[D♭ dTC] 2 [G LTC]

G jazz altered

[G dTC] 2 [D♭ LTC]

D♭ Lydian dominant

[D♭ LTC] 0 [G dTC]

G half-whole diminished

[G dTC] 2 [D♭ dTC]

D♭ half-whole diminished

[D♭ dTC] 2 [G dTC]

G whole-tone

[G LTC] 0 [D♭ LTC]

D♭ whole-tone

[D♭ LTC] 0 [G LTC]

♭9	A♭	5
♭7	F	3
3	B	♭7
G7♭9		**D♭7**

G jazz altered

[G dTC] 2 [D♭ LTC]

D♭ Lydian dominant

[D♭ LTC] 0 [G dTC]

G half-whole diminished

[G dTC] 2 [D♭ dTC]

D♭ half-whole diminished

[D♭ dTC] 2 [G dTC]

9	A	♯5
♭7	F	3
3	B	♭7
G9		**D♭7♯5**

G Lydian dominant

[G LTC] 0 [D♭ dTC]

D♭ jazz altered

[D♭ dTC] 2 [G LTC]

G whole-tone

[G LTC] 0 [D♭ LTC]

D♭ whole-tone

[D♭ LTC] 0 [G LTC]

♯9	B♭	13
♭7	F	3
3	B	♭7

G7♯9   **D♭13**

G jazz altered

[G dTC] 2 [D♭ LTC]

D♭ Lydian dominant

[D♭ LTC] 0 [G dTC]

G half-whole diminished

[G dTC] 2 [D♭ dTC]

D♭ half-whole diminished

[D♭ dTC] 2 [G dTC]

Part Two: Four-Note Voicings

1	G	♭5			
♭5	D♭	1			
3	B	♭7			
♭7	F	3			
G7♭5			**D♭7♭5**		

G Lydian dominant

[G LTC] 0 [D♭ dTC]

D♭ jazz altered

[D♭ dTC] 2 [G LTC]

G jazz altered

[G dTC] 2 [D♭ LTC]

D♭ Lydian dominant

[D♭ LTC] 0 [G dTC]

G half-whole diminished

[G dTC] 2 [D♭ dTC]

D♭ half-whole diminished

[D♭ dTC] 2 [G dTC]

G whole-tone

[G LTC] 0 [D♭ LTC]

D♭ whole-tone

[D♭ LTC] 0 [G LTC]

♭9	A♭	5
♭5	D♭	1
3	B	♭7
♭7	F	3
G7♭5♭9		**D♭7**

G jazz altered
[G dTC] 2 [D♭ LTC]

D♭ Lydian dominant
[D♭ LTC] 0 [G dTC]

G half-whole diminished
[G dTC] 2 [D♭ dTC]

D♭ half-whole diminished
[D♭ dTC] 2 [G dTC]

9	A	♯5
♭5	D♭	1
3	B	♭7
♭7	F	3
G9♭5		**D♭7♯5**

G Lydian dominant
[G LTC] 0 [D♭ dTC]

D♭ jazz altered
[D♭ dTC] 2 [G LTC]

G whole-tone
[G LTC] 0 [D♭ LTC]

D♭ whole-tone
[D♭ LTC] 0 [G LTC]

#9	Bb	13
b5	Db	1
3	B	b7
b7	F	3
G7b5#9		**Db13**

G jazz altered
[G dTC] 2 [Db LTC]

Db Lydian dominant
[Db LTC] 0 [G dTC]

G half-whole diminished
[G dTC] 2 [Db dTC]

Db half-whole diminished
[Db dTC] 2 [G dTC]

1	G	b5
5	D	b9
3	B	b7
b7	F	3
G7		**Db7b5b9**

G Lydian dominant
[G LTC] 0 [Db dTC]

Db jazz altered
[Db dTC] 2 [G LTC]

G half-whole diminished
[G dTC] 2 [Db dTC]

Db half-whole diminished
[Db dTC] 2 [G dTC]

♭9	A♭	5
5	D	♭9
3	B	♭7
♭7	F	3
G7♭9		**D♭7♭9**

G half-whole diminished
[G dTC] 2 [D♭ dTC]

D♭ half-whole diminished
[D♭ dTC] 2 [G dTC]

9	A	♯5
5	D	♭9
3	B	♭7
♭7	F	3
G9		**D♭7♯5♭9**

G Lydian dominant
[G LTC] 0 [D♭ dTC]

D♭ jazz altered
[D♭ dTC] 2 [G LTC]

♯9	B♭	13
5	D	♭9
3	B	♭7
♭7	F	3
G7♯9		**D♭13♭9**

G half-whole diminished
[G dTC] 2 [D♭ dTC]

D♭ half-whole diminished
[D♭ dTC] 2 [G dTC]

124

1	G	♭5
♯5	E♭	9
3	B	♭7
♭7	F	3

G7♯5   D♭9♭5

G jazz altered
[G dTC] 2 [D♭ LTC]

D♭ Lydian dominant
[D♭ LTC] 0 [G dTC]

G whole-tone
[G LTC] 0 [D♭ LTC]

D♭ whole-tone
[D♭ LTC] 0 [G LTC]

♭9	A♭	5
♯5	E♭	9
3	B	♭7
♭7	F	3

G7♯5b9   D♭9

G jazz altered
[G dTC] 2 [D♭ LTC]

D♭ Lydian dominant
[D♭ LTC] 0 [G dTC]

9	A	♯5
♯5	E♭	9
3	B	♭7
♭7	F	3

G9♯5   D♭9♯5

G whole-tone
[G LTC] 0 [D♭ LTC]

D♭ whole-tone
[D♭ LTC] 0 [G LTC]

125

#9	Bb	13
#5	Eb	9
3	B	b7
b7	F	3

G7#5#9   **Db13**

G jazz altered
[G dTC] 2 [Db LTC]

Db Lydian dominant
[Db LTC] 0 [G dTC]

1	G	b5
13	E	#9
3	B	b7
b7	F	3

G13   **Db7b5#9**

G Lydian dominant
[G LTC] 0 [Db dTC]

Db jazz altered
[Db dTC] 2 [G LTC]

G half-whole diminished
[G dTC] 2 [Db dTC]

Db half-whole diminished
[Db dTC] 2 [G dTC]

----

b9	Ab	5
13	E	#9
3	B	b7
b7	F	3

G13b9   **Db7#9**

G half-whole diminished
[G dTC] 2 [Db dTC]

Db half-whole diminished
[Db dTC] 2 [G dTC]

9	A	#5
13	E	#9
3	B	♭7
♭7	F	3
G13		**D♭7#5#9**

G Lydian dominant
[G LTC] 0 [D♭ dTC]

D♭ jazz altered
[D♭ dTC] 2 [G LTC]

#9	B♭	13
13	E	#9
3	B	♭7
♭7	F	3
G13#9		**D♭13#9**

G half-whole diminished
[G dTC] 2 [D♭ dTC]

D♭ half-whole diminished
[D♭ dTC] 2 [G dTC]

Part Three

$\flat 5$ D$\flat$ 1

1   G $\flat 5$

$\flat 7$ F   3

3   B $\flat 7$

G7$\flat$5   **D$\flat$7$\flat$5**

G Lydian dominant

[G LTC] 0 [D$\flat$ dTC]

D$\flat$ jazz altered

[D$\flat$ dTC] 2 [G LTC]

G jazz altered

[G dTC] 2 [D$\flat$ LTC]

D$\flat$ Lydian dominant

[D$\flat$ LTC] 0 [G dTC]

G half-whole diminished

[G dTC] 2 [D$\flat$ dTC]

D$\flat$ half-whole diminished

[D$\flat$ dTC] 2 [G dTC]

G whole-tone

[G LTC] 0 [D$\flat$ LTC]

D$\flat$ whole-tone

[D$\flat$ LTC] 0 [G LTC]

5	D	♭9
1	G	♭5
♭7	F	3
3	B	♭7
G7		**D♭7♭5♭9**

G Lydian dominant
[G LTC] 0 [D♭ dTC]

D♭ jazz altered
[D♭ dTC] 2 [G LTC]

G half-whole diminished
[G dTC] 2 [D♭ dTC]

D♭ half-whole diminished
[D♭ dTC] 2 [G dTC]

♯5	E♭	9
1	G	♭5
♭7	F	3
3	B	♭7
G7♯5		**D♭9♭5**

G jazz altered
[G dTC] 2 [D♭ LTC]

D♭ Lydian dominant
[D♭ LTC] 0 [G dTC]

G whole-tone
[G LTC] 0 [D♭ LTC]

D♭ whole-tone
[D♭ LTC] 0 [G LTC]

13	E	♯9
1	G	♭5
♭7	F	3
3	B	♭7
G13		**D♭7♭5♯9**

G Lydian dominant
[G LTC] 0 [D♭ dTC]

D♭ jazz altered
[D♭ dTC] 2 [G LTC]

G half-whole diminished
[G dTC] 2 [D♭ dTC]

D♭ half-whole diminished
[D♭ dTC] 2 [G dTC]

♭5	D♭	1
♭9	A♭	5
♭7	F	3
3	B	♭7
G7♭5♭9		**D♭7**

G jazz altered
[G dTC] 2 [D♭ LTC]

D♭ Lydian dominant
[D♭ LTC] 0 [G dTC]

G half-whole diminished
[G dTC] 2 [D♭ dTC]

D♭ half-whole diminished
[D♭ dTC] 2 [G dTC]

5	D	♭9
♭9	A♭	5
♭7	F	3
3	B	♭7
G7♭9		**D♭7♭9**

G half-whole diminished
[G dTC] 2 [D♭ dTC]

D♭ half-whole diminished
[D♭ dTC] 2 [G dTC]

♯5	E♭	9
♭9	A♭	5
♭7	F	3
3	B	♭7
G7♯5♭9		**D♭9**

G jazz altered
[G dTC] 2 [D♭ LTC]

D♭ Lydian dominant
[D♭ LTC] 0 [G dTC]

13	E	♯9
♭9	A♭	5
♭7	F	3
3	B	♭7
G13♭9		**D♭7♯9**

G half-whole diminished
[G dTC] 2 [D♭ dTC]

D♭ half-whole diminished
[D♭ dTC] 2 [G dTC]

131

♭5	D♭	1
9	A	♯5
♭7	F	3
3	B	♭7
G9♭5		**D♭7♯5**

G Lydian dominant
[G LTC] 0 [D♭ dTC]

D♭ jazz altered
[D♭ dTC] 2 [G LTC]

G whole-tone
[G LTC] 0 [D♭ LTC]

D♭ whole-tone
[D♭ LTC] 0 [G LTC]

5	D	♭9
9	A	♯5
♭7	F	3
3	B	♭7
G9		**D♭7♯5D♭9**

G Lydian dominant
[G LTC] 0 [D♭ dTC]

D♭ jazz altered
[D♭ dTC] 2 [G LTC]

♯5	E♭	9
9	A	♯5
♭7	F	3
3	B	♭7
G9♯5		**D♭9♯5**

G whole-tone
[G LTC] 0 [D♭ LTC]

D♭ whole-tone
[D♭ LTC] 0 [G LTC]

13	E	♯9
9	A	♯5
♭7	F	3
3	B	♭7

G13   **D♭7♯5♯9**

G Lydian dominant
[G LTC] 0 [D♭ dTC]

D♭ jazz altered
[D♭ dTC] 2 [G LTC]

♭5	D♭	1
♯9	B♭	13
♭7	F	3
3	B	♭7

G7♭5♯9   **D♭13**

G jazz altered
[G dTC] 2 [D♭ LTC]

D♭ Lydian dominant
[D♭ LTC] 0 [G dTC]

G half-whole diminished
[G dTC] 2 [D♭ dTC]

D♭ half-whole diminished
[D♭ dTC] 2 [G dTC]

5	D	♭9
♯9	B♭	13
♭7	F	3
3	B	♭7

G7♯9   **D♭13♭9**

G half-whole diminished
[G dTC] 2 [D♭ dTC]

D♭ half-whole diminished
[D♭ dTC] 2 [G dTC]

♯5	E♭	9
♯9	B♭	13
♭7	F	3
3	B	♭7
G7♯5♯9		**D♭13**

G jazz altered

[G dTC] 2 [D♭ LTC]

D♭ Lydian dominant

[D♭ LTC] 0 [G dTC]

13	E	♯9
♯9	B♭	13
♭7	F	3
3	B	♭7
G13♯9		**D♭13♯9**

G half-whole diminished

[G dTC] 2 [D♭ dTC]

D♭ half-whole diminished

[D♭ dTC] 2 [G dTC]

Approaching Chord Tones

You've got a chord with 4 or more notes in it.

Any of those chord tones, by definition, are going to be consonant with that underlying chord.

The question then becomes, *"Which melody notes can go in between the chord tones, and how can I melodically approach those chord tones?"*

The vast majority of chord tones are either a minor third or a major third apart.

If you want to move from one chord tone to another chord tone a minor third away you have several choices:

1. Use one or the other chromatics as a passing tone

ascending
C D E♭
C D♭ E♭

descending
E♭ D C
E♭ D♭ C

2. Use both chromatics as passing tones

ascending
C C♯ D E♭

descending
E♭ D D♭ C

3. Approach the target note using the surrounding note figure "SNF"
(aka enclosure / encirclement)

whole step
C F E♭

half-step
C E E♭

whole-step
E♭ B♭ C

half-step
E♭ B C

4. Compound SNFs

half steps
C E D E♭

E♭ B D♭ C

whole steps
C F D♭ E♭

E♭ B♭ D C

W-h combos
C F D E♭

C E D♭ E♭

E♭ B♭ D♭ C

E♭ B D C

What would influence your note choices in these situations?

First and foremost, your ear and good taste. Secondly, know which of these approach notes are in the current underlying tonality. Often it's a good idea to tip your hat to the underlying tonality. Also keep in mind that half-step approaches are generally stronger than whole-step approaches.

There exist similar situations with chord tones that are a major third apart.

There are three chromatics between chord tones a major third apart.

1. Use one of the chromatics as a passing tone

ascending
C D♯ E
C D E
C D♭ E

descending
E D♯ C
E D C
E D♭ C

2. Use two of the chromatics as passing tones

ascending
C D D♯ E
C C♯ D E
C C♯ D♯ E (diminished tetrachord)

descending
E E♭ D C
E D D♭ C
E E♭ D♭ C (diminished tetrachord)

3. Use all three of the chromatics as passing tones

ascending
C C♯ D D♯ E

descending
E E♭ D D♭ C

4. Surrounding Note Figures

simple
C F E
C F♯ E

E B C
E B♭ C

compound
C F D♯ E
C F D E
C F♯ D♯ E
C F♯ D E

E B D♭ C
E B♭ D♭ C
E B D C
E B♭ D C

Once again, you might want to take into account the underlying current tonality, but above all USE YOUR EARS!

Temporal Considerations and Harmonic Rhythm

Consider this concept: Play a C major chord on the harmonic instrument of your choice for a day. Follow this by playing an F chord for another day. While you are playing the C for a day, what key are you in? C major, of course, and while you are playing the F for the day? F major.

Now repeat this same process, but in 12-hour segments: C for 12 hours, then F for another 12. Then six hours each, and then three. Continue this "lessening" process until you have around two measures for each chord. Somewhere along the way, your musical sense will assign one key or the other to both chords, and for two beats each at medium to up tempo, the ear will easily perceive one or the other as the predominant chord or key.

At what point exactly does this perception of predominant key begin? Playing a chord for several hours removes the previous chord from consideration for melodic composition and improvisation, but at two beats each, one has no trouble at all reacting to both chords as being from a single "tonality". What about two measures each? Four, eight, sixteen, etc …?

Harmonic rhythm is one of the single most important concepts for the student of music to grasp.

It cannot be quantified as to how long a chord must last in order for the next one or the previous one to be either predominant or subordinate. You may either react to chords in the prevailing harmonic environment one at a time (locally), or in groups of two or more (globally), and it is easily observed that certain chords exert more influence than others, such as the I chord resolution in the ubiquitous ii-V7-I progression.

Further, there are even times you may choose to react to chords that aren't even there (here this is called an "imaginary" chord progression).

Examples over the chord progression Dm7 G7♯9 Cmaj7:

Local:

Play D Dorian over the Dm7, the G half-whole diminished scale over the G7♯9, and C Lydian over the Cmaj7 chord.

Global:

Play a C major scale over the entire progression.

Imaginary:

Play a G♭ major scale over the entire progression. This might seem "out there," until it is seen that G♭ major serves as a tritone substitute for the altered G7 chord.

Inversions of Type 1 Perfect Chords

F Lydian is the pitch set identical to the perfect Fmaj13#11 chord, consequently it is a completely valid scale option for melodic use over the inversions of the Fmaj7 tetrad:

Fmaj7   Fmaj7/A   Fmaj7/C   Fmaj7/E

F Lydian is also the relative major of D Dorian, which is the pitch set identical to the perfect Dm13 chord; therefore, it is also a valid scale option for melodic use over inversions of the Dm7 tetrad:

Dm7   Dm7/F   Dm7/A   Dm7/C

Note that the tonic of the relative major chord (F) is the ♭3 of the minor chord. This is important as its *"differentiating tone."* In other words, the tone that defines the quality of the minor triad is the tonic of its relative major chord.

The differentiating tone of the minor triad is the tonic of the scale of
the perfect major chord: <u>the Lydian scale</u>.

There are two other chord types found in the heptatonic ur-scale: the dominant seventh chord and the half-diminished seventh chord.

The differentiating tone of the dominant seventh chord (ie. the one tone that differentiates it from the major seventh chord) is its flat seventh.

The differentiating tone of the half-diminished seventh chord (ie. the one tone that differentiates it from the minor seventh chord) is its flat fifth.

The differentiating tones of the dominant and half-diminished chords are the tonics of a type of perfect scale for these chords: the Lydian scale.

G7 (extended to include Fmaj13#11)

G	B	D	**F**	**A**	**C**	**E**	**G**	**B**	**D**
1	3	5	♭7	9	11	13	1	3	5

or in stepwise order:

G   A   B   C   D   E   F   G

which is a G Mixolydian scale
(2nd mode of F Lydian / 5th mode of C major)

Bm7♭5 (extended to include Fmaj13#11)

B	D	F	A	C	E	G	B	D
1	♭3	♭5	♭7	♭9	11	♭13	1	♭3

or in stepwise order:

B   C   D   E   F   G   A   B

which is a B locrian scale

(#4th mode of F Lydian / 7th mode of C major)

How can this be useful?

In a local harmonic environment, one approach is to determine the differentiating tone and then play its corresponding lydian scale. Examples:

Chord	Differentiating Tone	Relative Lydian Scale	Ionian Set Mode
Fmaj7	Root (F)	F Lydian	F Lydian
Dm7	♭3 (F)	F Lydian	D Dorian
Bm7♭5	♭5 (F)	F Lydian	B Locrian
G7	♭7 (F)	F Lydian	G Mixolydian
Fmaj7	Root (F)	F Lydian	F Lydian
Fm7	♭3 (A♭)	A♭ Lydian	F Dorian
Fm7♭5	♭5 (B)	B Lydian	F Locrian
F7	♭7 (E♭)	E♭ Lydian	F Mixolydian

These substitutions may be used to find a scale that fits the sound of the individual chords.

There are four chord types, each with four inversions resulting in a total of sixteen permutations for every single heptatonic ur-scale. Notice how they overlap.

Example in F Lydian:

Bass Note	Chords and their Inversions			
F	Fmaj7	Dm7/F	Bm7♭5/F	G7/F
G				G7
A	Fmaj7/A	Dm7/A	Bm7♭5/A	
B			Bm7♭5	G7/B
C	Fmaj7/C	Dm7/C		
D		Dm7	Bm7♭5/D	G7/D
E	Fmaj7/E			

141

Minor Scale Chord Tables

These tables are arranged in the order of the "circular minor chord sequences table" in the chapter on minor scales (pg 54).

In theory, a chord built off any scale degree will lead to any other chord in the next chord family that is a fourth above the previous chord and so on. (In reality, though, you'll have to use good taste.)

With the interchangeability of the different chords built off each degree, the theoretical possibility of 302,400 chord combinations exists. Plenty enough to satisfy the most creative mind.

Explanation of symbols used in the tables:
"ivD" indicates that this chord is built off the **fourth** degree of the Dorian.
"**A**" indicates "Aeolian", "**H**" = "Harmonic", "**M**" = "Melodic"

Chords Built off the Fourth Degrees

Table 4.3: Triads built off the fourth degrees

Major	ivD			ivM
minor		ivA	ivH	
Sus4	ivD	ivA		
Sus2	ivD	ivA	ivH	ivM
diminished			ivH	

Table 4.4: Four-note chords built off the fourth degrees

7th	ivD			ivM
m7		ivA	ivH	
7sus4	ivD	ivA		
m7♭5			ivH	
7♭5				ivM

Table 4.5: Five-note chords built off the fourth degrees

9th	ivD			ivM
m9		ivA	ivH	
Maj69	ivD			ivM
m69		ivA	ivH	
9sus4	ivD	ivA		
9♭5				ivM
m9♭5			ivH	

Chords Built off the Flat Seventh Degrees

Table ♭7.3: Triads built off the ♭7 degrees

Major	♭viiD	♭viiA		
sus2	♭viiD	♭viiA		
sus4	♭viiD	♭viiA		

Table ♭7.4: Four-note chords built off the ♭7 degrees

Maj6	♭viiD	♭viiA		
Maj7	♭viiD			
7th		♭viiA		
Maj7sus4	♭viiD			
7sus4		♭viiA		

Table ♭7.5: Five-note chords built off the ♭7 degrees

Maj9	♭viiD			
9th		♭viiA		
Maj69	♭viiD	♭viiA		
9(add6)		♭viiA		

Chords Built off the Flat Third Degrees

Table ♭3.3: Triads built off the ♭3 degrees

Major	♭iiiD	♭iiiA		
Augmented			♭iiiH	♭iiiM
sus4		♭iiiA		
sus2	♭iiiD	♭iiiA		

Table ♭3.4: Four-note chords built off the ♭3 degrees

Maj7	♭iiiD	♭iiiA		
Maj7♯5			♭iiiH	♭iiiM
Maj6	♭iiiD	♭iiiA		
Maj7sus4		♭iiiA		

Table ♭3.5: Five-note chords built off the ♭3 degrees

Maj9	♭iiiD	♭iiiA		
Maj9♯5			♭iiiH	♭iiiM
Maj69	♭iiiD	♭iiiA		

Chords Built off the Sixth Degrees

Table 6.3: Triads built off the 6th degrees

diminished	viD			viM

Table 6.4: Four-note chords built off the 6th degrees

m7♭5	viD			viM

Table 6.5: Five-note chords built off the 6th degrees

m7♭5♭9	viD			
m9♭5				viM

Chords Built off the Lowered Sixth Degrees

Table ♭6.3: Triads built off the ♭6 degrees

Major		♭viA	♭viH	
sus4		♭viA		
diminished			♭viH	

Table ♭6.4: Four-note chords built off the ♭6 degrees

Maj7		♭viA	♭viH	
dim7			♭viH	

Table ♭6.5: Five-note chords built off the ♭6 degrees

Maj9		♭viA		
Maj7♯9			♭viH	

Chords Built off the Second Degrees

Table 2.3: Triads built off the 2nd degrees

minor	iiD			iiM
diminished		iiA	iiH	
sus4	iiD			iiM

Table 2.4: Four-note chords built off the 2nd degrees

m6				iiM
m7	iiD			iiM
m7♭5		iiA	iiH	
dim7			iiH	
7sus4	iiD			iiM

Table 2.5: Five-note chords built off the 2nd degrees

m7♭9	iiD			iiM
m7♭5♭9		iiA	iiH	
m6♭9				iiM
dim7♭9			iiH	

Chords Built off the Fifth Degrees

Table 5.3: Triads built off the 5th degrees

minor	vD	vA		
Major			vH	vM
sus4	vD	vA	vH	vM
sus2	vD			vM
Augmented			vH	vM

Table 5.4: Four-note chords built off the 5th degrees

m7	vD	vA		
7th			vH	vM
7sus4	vD	vA	vH	vM
7♯5			vH	vM

Table 5.5: Five-note chords built off the 5th degrees

m9	vD			
m7♭9		vA		
7♭9			vH	
9th				vM
7♯5♭9			vH	
9♯5				vM

Chords Built off the Raised Seventh Degrees

Table ♮7.3: Triads built off the ♮7 degrees

Diminished			♮viiH	♮viiM
Augmented			♮viiH	♮viiM

Table ♮7.4: Four-note chords built off the ♮7 degrees

dim7			♮viiH	
m7♭5				♮viiM
7♯5				♮viiM

Table ♮7.5: Five-note chords built off the ♮7 degrees

dim7♭9			♮viiH	
m7♭5♭9				♮viiM
7♯5♭9				♮viiM

Chords Built off the First Degrees

Table 1.3: Triads built off the 1st degrees

minor	iD	iA	iH	iM
sus2	iD	iA	iH	iM
sus4	iD	iA	iH	iM

Table 1.4: Four-note chords built off the 1st degrees

m6	iD			iM
m7	iD	iA		
mM7			iH	iM
7sus4	iD	iA		

Table 1.5: Five-note chords built off the 1st degrees

m69	iD			iM
m9	iD	iA		
mM9			iH	iM
9sus4	iD	iA	iH	iM

Cross-Referenced Minor Scale Chord Tables

The following set of tables lists each chord type, the scale and scale degree the chord was derived from

It also strongly implies that a plausible scale choice for improvising over said chord would be the scale it was derived from.

Example:

Augmented			♮viiH	♮viiM
Augmented			♭iiiH	♭iiiM
Augmented			vH	vM

The above table indicates that an Augmented triad can be built off:

the ♮7th degree of the harmonic minor scale,

the ♮7th degree of the melodic minor scale,

the ♭3rd degree of the harmonic minor scale,

the ♭3rd degree of the melodic minor scale,

the 5th degree of the harmonic minor scale,

the 5th degree of the melodic minor scale.

An augmented triad built off the ♮7th degree of either the harmonic minor scale or melodic minor scale in the key of A minor would be "**G♯♯+**".

In the key of A minor, the scale built off the ♮7th degree of the harmonic minor scale is:
G♯ A B C D E F G♯

In the key of A minor, the scale built off the ♮7th degree of the melodic minor is:
G♯ A B C D E F♯ G♯

An augmented triad built off the ♭3rd degree of either the harmonic minor scale or melodic minor scale in the key of A minor would be "**C+**".

In the key of A minor, the scale built off the ♭3rd degree of the harmonic minor scale is:
C D E F G♯ A B C

In the key of A minor, the scale built off the ♭3rd degree of the melodic minor scale is:
C D E F♯ G♯ A B C

An augmented triad built off the 5th degree of either the harmonic minor scale or melodic minor scale in the key of A minor would be "**E+**".

In the key of A minor, the scale built off the 5th degree of the harmonic minor scale is:
E F G♯ A B C D E

In the key of A minor, the scale built off the 5th degree of the melodic minor is:
E F♯ G♯ A B C D E

(Note: Scales built off the various degrees of the Dorian and Aeolian modes have specific and commonly accepted names. Scales built off the various degrees of the harmonic minor and melodic minor scales do not all have names, and many of the names are either not commonly accepted or understood by all. Therefore, degrees and root scale names are simply assigned to ALL of them for the sake of consistency and in order to avoid confusion.)

Triads Table

Augmented			♮viiH	♮viiM
Augmented			♭iiiH	♭iiiM
Augmented			vH	vM
diminished			ivH	
diminished			♮viiH	♮viiM
diminished			♭viH	
diminished	viD			viM
diminished		iiA	iiH	
Major	ivD			ivM
Major	♭viiD	♭viiA		
Major	♭iiiD	♭iiiA		
Major		♭viA	♭viH	
Major			vH	vM
minor		ivA	ivH	
minor	iiD			iiM
minor	vD	vA		
minor	iD	iA	iH	iM
sus2	ivD	ivA	ivH	ivM
sus2	♭viiD	♭viiA		
sus2	♭iiiD	♭iiiA		
sus2	vD			vM
sus2	iD	iA	iH	iM
sus4	ivD	ivA		
sus4	♭viiD	♭viiA		
sus4		♭iiiA		
sus4		♭viA		
sus4	iiD			iiM
sus4	vD	vA	vH	vM
sus4	iD	iA	iH	iM

4-Note Chords Table

7♯5				♮viiM
7♯5			vH	vM
7♭5				ivM
7sus4	ivD	ivA		
7sus4		♭viiA		
7sus4	iiD			iiM
7sus4	vD	vA	vH	vM
7sus4	iD	iA		
7th	ivD			ivM
7th		♭viiA		
7th			vH	vM
dim7			♮viiH	
dim7			♭viH	
dim7			iiH	
m6				iiM
m6	iD			iM
m7		ivA	ivH	
m7	iiD			iiM
m7	vD	vA		
m7	iD	iA		
m7♭5			ivH	
m7♭5				♮viiM
m7♭5	viD			viM
m7♭5		iiA	iiH	
Maj6	♭viiD	♭viiA		
Maj6	♭iiiD	♭iiiA		
Maj7	♭viiD			
Maj7	♭iiiD	♭iiiA		
Maj7		♭viA	♭viH	
Maj7♯5			♭iiiH	♭iiiM
Maj7sus4	♭viiD			
Maj7sus4		♭iiiA		
mM7			iH	iM

5-Note Chords Table

7#5b9				♮viiM
7#5b9			vH	
7b9			vH	
9#5				vM
9(add6)		bviiA		
9b5				ivM
9sus4	ivD	ivA		
9sus4	iD	iA	iH	iM
9th	ivD			ivM
9th		bviiA		
9th				vM
dim7b9			♮viiH	
dim7b9			iiH	
m69		ivA	ivH	
m69	iD			iM
m6b9				iiM
m7b5b9				♮viiM
m7b5b9	viD			
m7b5b9		iiA	iiH	
m7b9	iiD			iiM
m7b9		vA		
m9		ivA	ivH	
m9	vD			
m9	iD	iA		
m9b5			ivH	
m9b5				viM
Maj69	ivD			ivM
Maj69	bviiD	bviiA		
Maj69	biiiD	biiiA		
Maj7#9			bviH	
Maj9	bviiD			
Maj9	biiiD	biiiA		
Maj9		bviA		
Maj9#5			biiiH	biiiM
mM9			iH	iM

Modes of the Jazz Minor

Jazz Minor

I		II		♭III		IV		V		VI		VII		I
	1		½		1		1		1		1		½	

figure 62

Jazz Phrygian (relative)

II		♭III		IV		V		VI		VII		I		II
	½		1		1		1		1		½		1	

figure 63

Jazz Phrygian (parallel)

I		♭II		♭III		IV		V		VI		♭VII		I
	½		1		1		1		1		½		1	

figure 64

Lydian Augmented (relative)

♭III		IV		V		VI		VII		I		II		♭III
	1		1		1		1		½		1		½	

figure 65

Lydian Augmented (parallel)

I		II		III		♯IV		♯V		VI		VII		I
	1		1		1		1		½		1		½	

figure 66

Lydian Dominant (relative)

IV		V		VI		VII		I		II		♭III		IV
	1		1		1		½		1		½		1	

figure 67

Lydian Dominant (parallel)

I		II		III		♯IV		V		VI		♭VII		I
	1		1		1		½		1		½		1	

figure 68

Jazz Mixolydian (relative)

V		VI		VII		I		II		♭III		IV		V
	1		1		½		1		½		1		1	

figure 69

Jazz Mixolydian (parallel)

I		II		III		IV		V		♭VI		♭VII		I
	1		1		½		1		½		1		1	

figure 70

Aeolian Diminished (relative)

VI		VII		I		II		♭III		IV		V		VI
	1		½		1		½		1		1		1	

figure 71

Aeolian Diminished (parallel)

I		II		♭III		IV		♭V		♭VI		♭VII		I
	1		½		1		½		1		1		1	

figure 72

Jazz Altered (relative)

VII		I		II		♭III		IV		V		VI		VII
	½		1		½		1		1		1		1	

figure 73

Jazz Altered (parallel)

I		♭II		♭III		♭IV		♭V		♭VI		♭VII		I
	½		1		½		1		1		1		1	

figure 74

Modes of the Harmonic Minor

Harmonic Minor / Aeolian ♮7 / Jazz Minor ♭6 / Mohammedan

I		II	♭III		IV		V	♭VI			VII	I

Jazz Phrygian Diminished / Locrian ♮6

I	♭II		♭III		IV	♭V			VI	♭VII		I

Ionian Augmented

I		II		III	IV			♯V	VI		VII	I

Romanian / Dorian ♯4 / Misheberakh

I		II	♭III			♯IV	V		VI	♭VII		I

Phrygian Dominant

I	♭II			III	IV		V	♭VI		♭VII		I

Lydian Blues Major / Lydian ♯2

I			♯II	III		♯IV	V		VI		VII	I

Leading Tone Minor Diminished / Superlocrian ♭♭7

I	♭II		♭III	♭IV		♭V		♭VI	♭♭VII			I

Modes of the Harmonic Major

Harmonic Major / Ionian ♭6

I		II	III	IV		V	♭VI			VII	I

Dorian ♭5

I		II	♭III		IV	♭V			VI	♭VII		I

Altered Phrygian Dominant / Phrygian ♭4 / Superlocrian ♮5 / Superphrygian

I	♭II		♭III	♭IV			V	♭VI		♭VII		I

Lydian Melodic Minor / Lydian ♭3 / Jazz Minor #4 / Lydian Diminished

I		II	♭III			#IV	V		VI		VII	I

Jazz Phrygian Dominant / Mixolydian ♭2

I	♭II			III	IV		V		VI	♭VII		I

Lydian Blues Augmented / Lydian Augmented #2

I			#II	III		#IV		#V	VI		VII	I

Leading Tone Major Diminished / Locrian ♭♭7 / Locrian Diminished 7

I	♭II		♭III		IV	♭V		♭VI	♭♭VII			I

ModeChords

Defining vs Non-Defining notes in the Heptatonic Modes

The following deals with how many notes are needed to unambiguously define the modes of the four most common heptatonic scales (ionian set, jazz minor set, harmonic minor set and harmonic major set),

When presented with either incomplete or garbled information (whether audio or visual), the human mind "fills in the gaps". When filling in those gaps, the mind automatically chooses the most obvious and common choices.

In this appendix chapter, this refers to the relationship between the notes in the first level of consonance of radial symmetry (a 4th above and a 4th below the central tonic note).

Completely analogous to chord construction, if the 5th is perfect it can almost always be omitted.

As such, a P5 is a non-defining note (both in chords and in modes).

If the 5th is altered (♭5 or ♯5), it then becomes a defining note and must (usually) be included.

Likewise, if the 4th is perfect it can also almost always be omitted.

If the 4th is altered (♭4 or ♯4), it then becomes a defining note and (usually) must be included.

The next consideration is whether a chromatic cluster might be created by the alteration of a note in the pitch set. Since this is "illegal" (in this discussion), chromatic clusters cannot be included in this study.

The final consideration is whether the absence of a note in a modechord will imply that one of the notes in the chord is something other than intended (ex. a chord with a ♯2 in it needs the M3 to establish that the ♯2 is NOT a m3).

The following analyses demonstrate that these modes may be unambiguously defined (in most cases) by chords containing less than six notes.

Ionian

Root

The root is a defining note by virtue of it being the *"home base"*.

Second

Here, the M2 cannot be lowered, because that creates a chromatic cluster between it and the ♮7 and root.

Also, the M2 cannot be raised, because that creates a chromatic cluster between it and the M3 and the P4.

As such, the M2 is a non-defining note in the Ionian because it is the only option possible.

Third

Here, the M3 is a defining note by virtue of its establishing that the mode is *"not minorish."*

Fourth*

The Ionian contains a P4, which by the above definition is non-defining.

Fifth

The Ionian contains a P5, which by the above definition is non-defining.

Sixth

Here, the ♮6 cannot be raised, because that creates a chromatic cluster between it and the ♮7 and root.

The ♮6 is a defining note by virtue of its establishing that the mode is *"not the harmonic major."*

Seventh

Here, the ♮7 is a defining note by virtue of its establishing that the mode is *"not Mixolydian."*

Summary of Ionian

Defining notes: Root, M3, ♮6, ♮7

Non-defining notes: M2, P4, P5

As such the mode can be unambiguously defined by a "**Maj13 chord (no 9, no 11)**."

*NB. in spite of the fact the P4 is the characteristic pitch, it is non-defining.

Dorian

Root

The root is a defining note by virtue of it being the "home base."

Second

Here, the second cannot be raised (♯2 = m3)

The second is a defining note by virtue of its establishing that the mode is *"not the 2nd mode of the jazz minor."*

Third

Here, the m3 is a defining note by virtue of its establishing that the mode is *"not majorish."*

Fourth

The Dorian contains a P4, which by the above definition is non-defining.

Fifth

The Dorian contains a P5, which by the above definition is non-defining.

Sixth

The ♮6 is a defining note by virtue of its establishing that the mode is *"not the Aeolian."*

Seventh

Here, the ♭7 is a defining note by virtue of its establishing that the mode is *"not the jazz minor."*

Summary of Dorian

Defining notes: root, M2, m3, ♮6, ♭7

Non-defining notes: P4, P5

As such the mode can be unambiguously defined by a "**m13 chord (no 11)**."

Phrygian

Root

The root is a defining note by virtue of it being the "home base."

Second

The ♭2 is a defining note by virtue of its establishing that the mode is *"not Aeolian."*

Third

Here, the m3 is a defining note by virtue of its establishing that the mode is *"not majorish."*

Fourth

The Phrygian contains a P4, which by the above definition is non-defining.

Fifth

The Phrygian contains a P5, which by the above definition is non-defining.

Sixth

Here, the ♭6 is a defining note by virtue of its establishing that the mode is *"not the 2nd mode of the jazz minor."*

Seventh

Here, the ♭7 cannot be raised, because that creates a chromatic cluster between it and the root and ♭2.

Also, the ♭7 cannot be lowered to become a dim7 interval from the root, because that creates a chromatic cluster between it and the P5 and the ♭6.

As such, it is a non-defining note in the Phrygian because it is the only option possible.

Summary of Phrygian

Defining notes: root, ♭2, m3, ♭6

Non-defining notes: P4, P5, ♭7

As such the mode can be unambiguously defined by a "**m♭9♭13 chord (no 7)**."

Lydian

Root

The root is a defining note by virtue of it being the "home base."

Second

Here, the M2 cannot be lowered, because that creates a chromatic cluster between it and the root and ♮7.

It is a defining note by virtue of its establishing that the mode is *"not the 4th mode of the harmonic major."*

Third

Here, the M3 is a defining note by virtue of its establishing that the mode is *"not minorish."*

Fourth

Here, the ♯4 is a defining note by virtue of its alteration establishing that the mode is *"not Ionian."*

Fifth

The Lydian contains a P5, which by the above definition is non-defining.

Sixth

Here, the ♮6 cannot be lowered, because that creates a chromatic cluster between it and the ♯4 and the P5.

Also, the ♮6 cannot be raised, because that creates a chromatic cluster between it and the ♮7 and the root.

As such, the ♮6 is a non-defining note in the Lydian because it is the only option possible.

Seventh

Here, the ♮7 is a defining note by virtue of establishing that the mode is *"not the 4th mode of the jazz minor."*

Summary of Lydian

Defining notes: root, M2, M3, ♯4, ♮7

Non-defining notes: P5, ♮6

As such the mode can be unambiguously defined by a "**Maj9♯11 chord**."

Mixolydian

Root

The root is a defining note by virtue of it being the "home base."

Second

Here, the M2 cannot be raised, because that creates a chromatic cluster between it and the M3 and P4.

The M2 is a defining note by virtue of its establishing that the mode is *"not the 5th mode of the harmonic major."*

Third

Here, the M3 is a defining note by virtue of its establishing that the mode is *"not minorish."*

Fourth

The Mixolydian contains a P4, which by the above definition is non-defining.

Fifth

The Mixolydian contains a P5, which by the above definition is non-defining.

In addition, the P5 cannot be lowered, because that creates a chromatic cluster between it and the M3 and the P4.

AND the P5 cannot be raised, because that creates a chromatic cluster between it and the ♮6 and ♭7.

As such, the P5 is a also non-defining note in the Mixolydian because it is the only option possible.

Sixth

Here, the ♮6 is a defining note by virtue of its establishing that the mode is *"not the 5th mode of the jazz minor."*

Seventh

Here, the ♭7 is a defining note by virtue of its establishing that the mode is *"not ionian."*

Summary of Mixolydian

Defining notes: root, M2, M3, ♮6, ♭7

Non-defining notes: P4, P5

As such the mode can be unambiguously defined by a "**13th chord (no 11)**."

Aeolian

Root

The root is a defining note by virtue of it being the "home base."

Second

Here, the M2 is a defining note by virtue of its establishing that the mode is *"not Phrygian."*

Third

Here, the m3 is a defining note by virtue of its establishing that the mode is *"not majorish."*

Fourth

The Aeolian contains a P4, which by the above definition is non-defining.

In addition, the P4 cannot be lowered, because that creates a chromatic cluster between it and the M2 and the m3.

AND the P4 cannot be raised, because that creates a chromatic cluster between it and the P5 and ♭6.

As such, the P4 is a also non-defining note in the Aeolian because it is the only option possible.

Fifth

Here the P5 is a defining note by virtue of its establishing that the mode is *"not the 6th mode of the jazz minor"* (in spite the P5 normally being non-defining).

Sixth

Here, the ♭6 is a defining note by virtue of its establishing that the mode is *"not Dorian."*

Seventh

Here, the ♭7 is a defining note by virtue of its establishing that the mode is *"not harmonic minor."*

Summary of Aeolian

Defining notes: root, M2, m3, P5, ♭6, ♭7

Non-defining note: P4

As such the mode can be unambiguously defined by a "**m9♭13 (no 11) chord**."

Locrian

Root

The root is a defining note by virtue of it being the "home base."

Second

Here, the ♭2 is a defining note by virtue of its establishing that the mode is *"not the 6th mode of the jazz minor."*

Third

Here, the m3 cannot be lowered, because that creates a chromatic cluster between it and the ♭2 and root.

Also, the m3 cannot be raised, because that creates a chromatic cluster between it and the ♭5 and the P4.

As such, the m3 is a non-defining note in the Locrian because it is the only option possible.

Fourth

The Locrian contains a P4, which by the above definition is non-defining.

Fifth

Here, the ♭5 is a defining note by virtue of its alteration establishing that the mode is *"not Phrygian."*

Sixth

Here, the ♭6 is a defining note by virtue of its establishing that the mode is *"not the 2nd mode of the harmonic minor."*

Seventh

Here, the ♭7 cannot be raised, because that creates a chromatic cluster between it and the root and ♭2.

It is a defining note in the locrian by virtue of its establishing that the mode is *"not the 7th mode of the harmonic major."*

Summary of Locrian

Defining notes: root, ♭2, ♭5, ♭6, ♭7

Non-defining notes: m3, P4

As such the mode can be unambiguously defined by a "**m7♭5♭9♭13 (no 3, no 11) chord**."

Jazz Minor aka Ascending Melodic Minor / Jazz Melodic Minor

Root

The root is a defining note by virtue of it being the "home base."

Second

Here, the M2 cannot be lowered, because that creates a chromatic cluster between it and the ♮7 and root.

Also, the M2 cannot be raised (♯2 = ♭3).

As such, the M2 is a non-defining note in the jazz minor because it is the only option possible.

Third

Here, the m3 is a defining note by virtue of its establishing that the mode is *"not majorish."*

Fourth

The jazz minor contains a P4, which by the above definition is non-defining.

Fifth

The jazz minor contains a P5, which by the above definition is non-defining.

Sixth

Here, the ♮6 cannot be raised, because that creates a chromatic cluster between it and the ♮7 and root.

The ♮6 is a defining note by virtue of its establishing that the mode is *"not the harmonic minor."*

Seventh

Here, the ♮7 is a defining note by virtue of its establishing that the mode is *"not Dorian."*

Summary of Jazz Minor

Defining notes: root, m3, ♮6, ♮7

Non-defining notes: M2, P4, P5

As such the mode can be unambiguously defined by a "**mM13 (no 9, no 11) chord.**"

Jazz Minor (2nd mode) aka Jazz Phrygian / Phrygian ♮6 / Dorian ♭2

Root

The root is a defining note by virtue of it being the "home base."

Second

Here, the ♭2 is a defining note by virtue of its establishing that the mode is *"not Dorian."*

Third

Here, the m3 is a defining note by virtue of its establishing that the mode is *"not the 5th mode of the harmonic major."*

Fourth

The 2nd mode of the jazz minor contains a P4, which by the above definition is non-defining.

Fifth

The 2nd mode of the jazz minor contains a P5, which by the above definition is non-defining.

Sixth

Here, the ♮6 is a defining note by virtue of its establishing that the mode is *"not Phrygian."*

Seventh

Here, the ♭7 cannot be raised, because that creates a chromatic cluster between it and the root and ♭2.

Also, the ♭7 cannot be lowered (♭♭7 = ♮6).

As such, the ♭7 is a non-defining note in 2nd mode of the jazz minor because it is the only option possible.

Summary of Jazz Minor (2nd mode)

Defining notes: root, ♭2, m3, ♮6

Non-defining notes: P4, P5, ♭7

As such the mode can be unambiguously defined by a "**m6♭9 chord**."

Jazz Minor (♭3rd mode) aka Lydian ♯5 / Lydian Augmented

Root

The root is a defining note by virtue of it being the "home base."

Second

The M2 cannot be lowered, because that creates a chromatic cluster between it and the root and ♮7.

Here, the M2 is a defining note by virtue of its establishing that the mode is *"not ♭6th mode of the harmonic major."*

Third

Here, the M3 is a defining note by virtue of its establishing that the mode is *"not minorish."* (Also that the mode is *"not a diminished scale minus one note."*)

Fourth

Here, the ♯4 is a defining note by virtue of its alteration establishing that the mode is *"not the 3rd mode of the harmonic minor."*

Fifth

Here, the ♯5 is a defining note by virtue of its alteration establishing that the mode is *"not Lydian."*

Sixth*

Here, the ♮6 cannot be raised, because that creates a chromatic cluster between it and the root and ♮7. Also, the ♮6 cannot be lowered (♭6 = ♯5).

As such, the ♮6 is a non-defining note in b3rd mode of the jazz minor because it is the only option possible.

Seventh*

Here, the ♮7 cannot be lowered, because that creates a chromatic cluster between it and the ♯5 and ♮6.

As such, the ♮7 is a non-defining note in ♭3rd mode of the jazz minor because it is the only option possible.

*NB. In order to unambiguously establish that the mode is *"not the wholetone scale,"* either the ♮6 or ♮7 must be present (but not necessarily both).

Summary of Jazz Minor (3rd mode)

Defining notes: root, M2, M3, ♯4, ♯5, ♮7 (or ♮6)

Non-defining note: ♮6 (or ♮7)

As such the mode can be unambiguously defined by a "**Maj9♯5♯11 chord**."

Jazz Minor (4th mode) aka Lydian ♭7 / Lydian Dominant

Root

The root is a defining note by virtue of it being the "home base."

Second

Here, the M2 is a defining note by virtue of its establishing that the mode is *"not a diminished scale minus a note."*

Third

Here, the M3 is a defining note by virtue of its establishing that the mode is *"not minorish."*

Fourth

Here, the ♯4 is a defining note by virtue of its alteration establishing that the mode is *"not Mixolydian."*

Fifth*

The 4th mode of the jazz minor contains a P5, which by the above definition is non-defining.

Sixth*

Here, the ♮6 cannot be lowered, because that creates a chromatic cluster between it and the ♯4 and P5.

Also, the ♮6 cannot be raised (♯6 = ♭7).

As such, the ♮6 is a non-defining note in 4th mode of the jazz minor because it is the only option possible.

Seventh

Here, the ♭7 is a defining note by virtue of its establishing that the mode is *"not Lydian."*

*NB. In order to unambiguously establish that the mode is *"not the wholetone scale,"* either the P5 or ♮6 must be present (but not necessarily both).

Summary of Jazz Minor (4th mode)

Defining notes: root, M2, M3, ♯4, ♮6 (or P5), ♭7

Non-defining note: P5 (or ♮6)

As such the mode can be unambiguously defined by either a "**9♯11 chord**" or a "**13♯11 chord**."

Jazz Minor (5th mode) aka Jazz Mixolydian / Mixolydian ♭6

Root

The root is a defining note by virtue of it being the "home base."

Second

Here, the M2 is a defining note by virtue of its establishing that the mode is *"not the 5th mode of the harmonic minor."*

Third

Here, the M3 is a defining note by virtue of its establishing that the mode is *"not minorish."*

Fourth*

The 5th mode of the jazz minor contains a P4, which by the above definition is non-defining.

Fifth*

The 5th mode of the jazz minor contains a P5, which by the above definition is non-defining.

Sixth

Here, the ♭6 is a defining note by virtue of its establishing that the mode is *"not Mixolydian."*

Seventh

Here, the ♭7 is a defining note by virtue of its establishing that the mode is *"not the harmonic major scale."*

*NB. In order to unambiguously establish that the mode is "not the wholetone scale", either the P4 or P5 must be present (but not necessarily both).

Summary of Jazz Minor (5th mode)

Defining notes: root, M2, M3, P5 (or P4), ♭6, ♭7

Non-defining notes: P4 (or P5)

As such the mode can be unambiguously defined by either a "**9♭13 (no 11) chord**" or an "**11♭13 chord**."

Jazz Minor (6th mode) aka Aeolian Diminished / Aeolian ♭5 / Locrian ♮2

Root

The root is a defining note by virtue of it being the "home base."

Second

Here, the M2 is a defining note by virtue of its establishing that the mode is *"not Locrian."*

Third*

Here, the m3 cannot be raised, because that creates a chromatic cluster between it and the P4 and ♭5.

As such, the m3 is a non-defining note in 6th mode of the jazz minor because it is the only option possible.

Fourth*

Here, the P4 cannot be lowered, because that creates a chromatic cluster between it and the M2 and m3.

Also, the P4 cannot be raised (♯4 = ♭5).

As such, the P4 is a non-defining note in 6th mode of the jazz minor because it is the only option possible.

Fifth

Here, the ♭5 is a defining note by virtue of its alteration establishing that the mode is *"not Aeolian."*

Sixth

Here, the ♭6 is a defining note by virtue of its establishing that the mode is *"not the 2nd mode of the harmonic major."*

Seventh

Here, the ♭7 is a defining note by virtue of its establishing that the mode is *"not a diminished scale minus a note."*

*NB. In order to unambiguously establish that the mode is *"not the wholetone scale,"* either the m3 or P4 must be present (but not necessarily both).

Summary of Jazz Minor (6th mode)

Defining notes: root, M2, m3 (or P4), ♭5, ♭6, ♭7

Non-defining note: P4 (or m3)

As such the mode can be unambiguously defined by either a "**m9♭5♭13 chord**" or a "**m11♭5♭13 (no 3rd) chord**."

Jazz Minor (7th mode) aka Jazz Altered / Locrian ♭4 / Superlocrian

Root

The root is a defining note by virtue of it being the "home base."

Second*

Here, the ♭2 cannot be raised, because that creates a chromatic cluster between it and the root and the m3. As such, the ♭2 is a non-defining note in 7th mode of the jazz minor because it is the only option possible.

Third*

Here, the m3 could not be lowered to become a dim3, because that creates a chromatic cluster between it and the root and the ♭2.

Also, the m3 cannot be raised (M3 = ♭4).

As such, the m3 is a non-defining note in 7th mode of the jazz minor because it is the only option possible.

Fourth

Here, the ♭4 is a defining note by virtue of its alteration establishing that the mode is *"not Locrian."*

Fifth

Here, the ♭5 is a defining note by virtue of its alteration establishing that the mode is *"not the 3rd mode of the harmonic major."*

Sixth

Here, the ♭6 is a defining note by virtue of its establishing that the mode is *"not a diminished scale minus a note."*

Seventh

Here, the ♭7 cannot be raised, because that creates a chromatic cluster between it and the root and the ♭2.

Here, the ♭7 is a defining note by virtue of its establishing that the mode is *"not the 7th mode of the harmonic major."*

*NB. In order to unambiguously establish that the mode is *"not the wholetone scale,"* either the ♭2 or m3 must be present.

However, if the m3 is not present, the ♭4 could be perceived as a M3; and if the ♭2 is not present, the m3 could be perceived as a ♯9 (♯2).

Summary of Jazz Minor (7th mode)

Defining notes: root, ♭2, m3, ♭4, ♭5, ♭6, ♭7

Non-defining notes: none

This mode cannot be unambiguously defined by less than all seven notes in the mode.

Harmonic Minor aka Aeolian ♮7

Root

The root is a defining note by virtue of it being the "home base".

Second

Here, the M2 cannot be lowered, because that creates a chromatic cluster between it and the root and the ♮7.

As such, the M2 is a non-defining note in harmonic minor because it is the only option possible.

Third

Here, the m3 is a defining note by virtue of its establishing that the mode is *"not majorish."*

Fourth

The harmonic minor contains a P4, which by the above definition is non-defining.

In addition, the P4 cannot be lowered, because that creates a chromatic cluster between it and the M2 and the m3.

AND the P4 cannot be raised, because that creates a chromatic cluster between it and the P5 and ♭6.

As such, the P4 is a also non-defining note in the harmonic minor because it is the only option possible.

Fifth*

The harmonic minor contains a P5, which by the above definition is non-defining.

Sixth

Here, the ♭6 is a defining note by virtue of its establishing that the mode is *"not jazz minor."*

Seventh

Here, the ♮7 is a defining note by virtue of its establishing that the mode is *"not Aeolian."*

*NB. If the P5 is not present, the ♭6 could be perceived as a ♯5.

Summary of Harmonic Minor

Defining notes: root, m3, P5, ♭6, ♮7

Non-defining notes: M2, P4

As such the mode can be unambiguously defined by a "**mM7♭13 (no 9, no 11) chord.**"

Harmonic Minor (2nd mode) aka Locrian ♮6

Root

The root is a defining note by virtue of it being the "home base."

Second

Here, the ♭2 is a defining note by virtue of its establishing that the mode is *"not the 2nd mode of the harmonic major."*

Third

Here, the m3 cannot be lowered to become a dim3, because that creates a chromatic cluster between it and the root and the ♭2.

Also, the m3 cannot be raised, because that creates a chromatic cluster between it and the P4 and the ♭5.

As such, the m3 is a non-defining note in 2nd mode of the harmonic minor because it is the only option possible.

Fourth

The 2nd mode of the harmonic minor contains a P4, is a defining note by virtue of its establishing that the mode is *"not a diminished scale minus a note."*

Fifth

Here, the ♭5 is a defining note by virtue of its alteration establishing that the mode is *"not the 2nd mode of the jazz minor."*

Sixth

Here, the ♮6 is a defining note by virtue of its establishing that the mode is *"not Locrian."*

Seventh

Here, the ♭7 cannot be raised, because that creates a chromatic cluster between it and the root and the ♭2.

Also, the ♭7 cannot be lowered (♭♭7 = ♮6).

As such, the ♭7 is a non-defining note in 2nd mode of the harmonic minor because it is the only option possible.

Summary of Harmonic Minor (2nd mode)

Defining notes: root, ♭2, P4, ♭5, ♮6

Non-defining notes: ♭3, ♭7

As such the mode can be unambiguously defined by a "**dim11♭9 chord**."

Harmonic Minor (♭3rd mode) aka Ionian ♯5

Root

The root is a defining note by virtue of it being the "home base."

Second

Here, the M2 could not be lowered, because that creates a chromatic cluster between it and the root and the ♮7. Also, the M2 could not be raised, because that creates a chromatic cluster between it the M3 and the P4.

As such, the M2 is a non-defining note in ♭3rd mode of the harmonic minor because it is the only option possible.

Third

Here, the M3 is a defining note by virtue of its establishing that the mode is *"not minorish,"* and also that it is *"not a diminished scale minus one note."*

Fourth

Here the P4 is a defining note by virtue of its establishing that the mode is *"not the ♭3rd mode of the jazz minor"* (in spite of the P4 normally being non-defining).

Fifth

Here, the ♯5 is a defining note by virtue of its establishing that the mode is *"not Ionian."*

Sixth*

Here, the ♮6 cannot be raised, because that creates a chromatic cluster between it and the ♮7 and the root. Also, the ♮6 cannot be lowered (♭6 = ♯5).

As such, the ♮6 is a non-defining note in ♭3rd mode of the harmonic minor because it is the only option possible.

Seventh

Here, the ♮7 cannot be lowered, because that creates a chromatic cluster between it and the ♮6 and the ♯5. As such, the ♮7 is a non-defining note in ♭3rd mode of the harmonic minor because it is the only option possible.

*NB. In order to avoid the implication that the mode is the harmonic major, the ♮6 must be present.

Summary of Harmonic Minor (♭3rd mode)

Defining notes: root, M3, P4, ♯5, ♮6

Non-defining notes: M2, ♮7

As such the mode can be unambiguously defined by a "**Maj13♯5 (no 7, no 9) chord.**"

Harmonic Minor (4th mode) aka Dorian ♯4

Root

The root is a defining note by virtue of it being the "home base."

Second

Here, the M2 cannot be raised (♯2 = ♭3)

The M2 is a defining note by virtue of its establishing that the mode is *"not a diminished scale minus a note."*

.

Third

Here, the m3 is a defining note by virtue of its establishing that the mode is *"not majorish."*

Fourth

Here, the ♯4 is a defining note by virtue of its alteration establishing that the mode is *"not Dorian."*

Fifth

The 4th mode of the harmonic minor contains a P5, which by the above definition is non-defining.

Sixth

Here, the ♮6 cannot be lowered, because that creates a chromatic cluster between it and the P5 and ♯4.

Also, the ♮6 cannot be raised (♯6 = ♭7).

As such, the ♮6 is a non-defining note in 4th mode of the harmonic minor because it is the only option possible.

Seventh

Here, the ♭7 is a defining note by virtue of its establishing that the mode is *"not the 4th mode of the harmonic major."*

Summary of Harmonic Minor (4th mode)

Defining notes: root, M2, m3, ♯4, ♭7

Non-defining notes: P5, ♮6

As such the mode can be unambiguously defined by a "**m9♯11 chord**."

Harmonic Minor (5th mode) aka Phrygian ♮3

Root

The root is a defining note by virtue of it being the "home base."

Second

Here, the ♭2 is a defining note by virtue of its establishing that the mode is *"not Mixolydian."*

Third

Here, the M3 is a defining note by virtue of its establishing that the mode is *"not minorish."*

Fourth*

The 5th mode of the harmonic minor contains a P4, which by the above definition is non-defining.

Fifth*

The 5th mode of the harmonic minor contains a P5, which by the above definition is non-defining.

Sixth

Here, the ♭6 is a defining note by virtue of its establishing that the mode is *"not the 5th mode of the harmonic major."*

Seventh

Here, the ♭7 cannot be raised, because that creates a chromatic cluster between it and the root and the ♭2.

Also, the ♭7 cannot be lowered to become a dim7, because that creates a chromatic cluster between it and the P5 and ♭6.

As such, the ♭7 is a non-defining note because it is the only option possible.

*NB. In order to avoid the implication that the mode is the 7th mode of the jazz minor scale, either the P4 or P5 (but not both) must be present.

Summary of Harmonic Minor (5th mode)

Defining notes: root, b2, M3, P5 (or P4), ♭6

Non-defining notes: P4 (or P5), ♭7

As such the mode can be unambiguously defined by a "**Major triad add ♭9, add ♭13**."

Harmonic Minor (♭6th mode) aka Lydian ♯2

Root

The root is a defining note by virtue of it being the "home base."

Second

Here, the ♯2 is a defining note by virtue of its establishing that the mode is *"not Lydian."*

Third*

Here, the M3 cannot be raised, because that creates a chromatic cluster between it and the ♯4 and the P5. Also, the M3 cannot be lowered (m3 = ♯2).

As such, the M3 is a non-defining note because it is the only option possible.

Fourth

Here, the ♯4 cannot be lowered, because that creates a chromatic cluster between it and the ♯2 and the M3. Also, the ♯4 cannot be raised (x4 = P5).

As such, the ♯4 is a non-defining note because it is the only option possible (in spite of its alteration).

Fifth

The ♭6th mode of the harmonic minor contains a P5, which by the above definition is non-defining.

Sixth

Here, the ♮6 cannot be lowered, because that creates a chromatic cluster between it and the ♯4 and the P5.

Also, the ♮6 cannot be raised, because that creates a chromatic cluster between it and the ♮7 and the root.

As such, the ♮6 is a non-defining note in the ♭6th mode of the harmonic minor because it is the only option possible.

Seventh

Here, the ♮7 is a defining note by virtue of establishing that the mode is *"not a diminished scale minus one note."*

*NB. If the M3 is not present, the ♯2 could be perceived as a m3.

Summary of Harmonic Minor (♭6th mode)

Defining notes: root, ♯2, M3, ♮7

Non-defining notes: ♯4, P5, ♮6

As such the mode can be unambiguously defined by a "**Maj7♯9 chord**."

Harmonic Minor (7th mode) aka Superlocrian ♭♭7

Root

The root is a defining note by virtue of it being the "home base."

Second*

Here, the ♭2 cannot be raised, because that creates a chromatic cluster between it and the ♭3 and the ♭4.

As such, the ♭2 is a non-defining note in the 7th mode of the harmonic minor because it is the only option possible.

Third*

Here, the m3 cannot be lowered, because that creates a chromatic cluster between it and the root and ♭2. Also, the m3 cannot be raised (M3 = ♭4).

As such, the m3 is a non-defining note in the 7th mode of the harmonic minor because it is the only option possible.

Fourth

Here, the ♭4 is a defining note by virtue of its alteration establishing that the mode is *"not the 7th mode of the harmonic major."*

Fifth

Here, the ♭5 cannot be lowered, because that creates a chromatic cluster between it and the ♭3 and ♭4.

Also, the ♭5 cannot be raised, because that creates a chromatic cluster between it and the ♭6 and ♭♭7.

As such, the ♭5 is a non-defining note in the 7th mode of the harmonic minor (in spite of its alteration) because it is the only option possible.

Sixth

Here, the ♭6 is a defining note by virtue of establishing that the mode is *"not a diminished scale minus one note."*

Seventh

Here, the ♭♭7 is a defining note by virtue of establishing that the mode is "not the 7th mode of the jazz minor."

*NB. If the ♭2 is not present, the m3 could be perceived as a ♯9 (♯2); and if the m3 is not present, the ♭4 could be perceived as a M3.

Summary of Harmonic Minor (7th mode)

Defining notes: root, ♭2, m3, ♭4, ♭6, ♭♭7

Non-defining note: ♭5

As such the mode can be unambiguously defined by a "**dim7♭9♭11♭13 (no ♭5) chord**."

Harmonic Major aka Ionian ♭6

Root

The root is a defining note by virtue of it being the "home base."

Second

Here, the M2 cannot be lowered, because that creates a chromatic cluster between it and the ♮7 and the root.

Also, the M2 cannot be raised, because that creates a chromatic cluster between it and the M3 and the P4.

As such, the M2 is a non-defining note in the harmonic major because it is the only option possible.

Third

Here, the M3 is a defining note by virtue of its establishing that the mode is *"not minorish."*

Fourth

The harmonic major contains a P4, which by the above definition is non-defining.

Fifth*

The harmonic major contains a P5, which by the above definition is non-defining.

Sixth

Here, the ♭6 is a defining note by virtue of its establishing that the mode is *"not Ionian."*

Seventh

Here, the ♮7 is a defining note by virtue of its establishing that the mode is *"not the 5th mode of the jazz minor."*

*NB. If the P5 is not present, the ♭6 could be perceived as a ♯5.

Summary of Harmonic Major

Defining notes: root, M3, P5, ♭6, ♮7

Non-defining notes: M2, P4

As such the mode can be unambiguously defined by a "**Maj7♭13 (no 9, no 11) chord**."

Harmonic Major (2nd mode) aka Dorian ♭5

Root

The root is a defining note by virtue of it being the "home base."

Second

Here, the M2 is a defining note by virtue of its establishing that the mode is *"not the 2nd mode of the harmonic minor."*

Third

Here, the ♭3 is a defining note by virtue of its establishing that the mode is *"not majorish."*

Fourth

The 2nd mode of the harmonic major contains a P4, which by the above definition is non-defining.

Fifth

Here, the ♭5 is a defining note by virtue of its alteration establishing that the mode is *"not Dorian."*

Sixth

Here, the ♮6 is a defining note by virtue of its alteration establishing that the mode is *"not the 6th mode of the jazz minor."*

Seventh

Here, the ♭7 is a defining note by virtue of its alteration establishing that the mode is *"not a diminished scale minus one note."*

Summary of Harmonic Major (2nd mode)

Defining notes: root, M2, ♭3, ♭5, ♮6, ♭7

Non-defining notes: P4

As such the mode can be unambiguously defined by a "**m13♭5 (no 11) chord**."

Harmonic Major (3rd mode)
aka Phrygian ♭4 / Superphrygian

Root

The root is a defining note by virtue of it being the "home base."

Second*

Here, the ♭2 cannot be raised, because that creates a chromatic cluster between it and the m3 and the ♭4. As such, the ♭2 is a non-defining note in the 3rd mode of the harmonic major because it is the only option possible.

Third*

Here, the m3 cannot be lowered, because that creates a chromatic cluster between it and the root and the ♭2. Also, the m3 cannot be raised (M3 = ♭4). As such, the m3 is a non-defining note in the 3rd mode of the harmonic major because it is the only option possible.

Fourth

Here, the ♭4 is a defining note by virtue of its alteration establishing that the mode is *"not Phrygian."*

Fifth*

The 3rd mode of the harmonic major contains a P5, which by the above definition is non-defining.

Sixth

Here, the ♭6 is a defining note by virtue of its establishing that the mode is *"not a diminished scale minus one note."*

Seventh

Here, the ♭7 cannot be raised, because that creates a chromatic cluster between it and the root and the ♭2.

Also, the ♭7 cannot be lowered, because that creates a chromatic cluster between it and the P5 and the ♭6.

As such, the ♭7 is a non-defining note in the 3rd mode of the harmonic major because it is the only option possible.

*NB. If the ♭2 is not present, the m3 could be perceived as a ♯9 (♯2); and if the m3 is not present, the ♭4 could be perceived as a M3. Also, if the P5 is not present, the b6 could be perceived as a ♯5.

Summary of Harmonic Major (3rd mode)

Defining notes: root, ♭2, m3, ♭4, P5, ♭6

Non-defining note: ♭7

As such the mode can be unambiguously defined by a "**Major triad add ♭9 ♯9 ♭13.**"

Harmonic Major (4th mode) aka Lydian ♭3

Root

The root is a defining note by virtue of it being the "home base."

Second*

Here, the M2 cannot be lowered, because that creates a chromatic cluster between it and the ♮7 and the root. Also, the M2 cannot be raised (♯2 = m3).

As such, the M2 is a non-defining note in the 4th mode of the harmonic major because it is the only option possible.

Third

Here, the m3 is a defining note by virtue of its establishing that the mode is *"not majorish."*

Fourth

Here, the ♯4 is a defining note by virtue of its alteration establishing that the mode is *"not jazz minor."*

Fifth**

The 4th mode of the harmonic major contains a P5, which by the above definition is non-defining.

Sixth

Here, the ♮6 cannot be raised, because that creates a chromatic cluster between it and the ♮7 and the root. Also, the ♮6 cannot be lowered, because that creates a chromatic cluster between it and the ♯4 and the P5.

As such, the ♮6 is a non-defining note in the 4th mode of the harmonic major because it is the only option possible.

Seventh

Here, the ♮7 is a defining note by virtue of its establishing that the mode is *"not the 4th mode of the harmonic minor."*

*The defining notes of this subset are enharmonically identical to the Hm♭3 and Hm5 subsets. In the case of inversions which might cause ambiguity, add the M2.

**If the P5 is not present, the ♯4 could be perceived as a ♭5.

Summary of Harmonic Major (4th mode)

Defining notes: root, m3, ♯4, P5, ♮7

Non-defining notes: M2, ♮6

As such the mode can be unambiguously defined by a "**mM7♯11 (no 9) chord**."

Harmonic Major (5th mode) aka Mixolydian ♭2

Root

The root is a defining note by virtue of it being the "home base."

Second

Here, the ♭2 is a defining note by virtue of its establishing that the mode is *"not Mixolydian."*

Third

Here, the M3 is a defining note by virtue of its establishing that the mode is *"not minorish"* (as well as *"not the 2nd mode of the jazz minor"*).

Fourth

The 5th mode of the harmonic major contains a P4, which by the above definition is non-defining.

Fifth

The 5th mode of the harmonic major contains a P5, which by the above definition is non-defining.

Sixth

Here, the ♮6 is a defining note by virtue of its establishing that the mode is *"not the 5th mode of the harmonic minor."*

Seventh

Here, the ♭7 cannot be raised, because that creates a chromatic cluster between it and the root and the ♭2.

Also, the ♭7 cannot be lowered (♭♭7 = ♮6).

As such, the ♭7 is a non-defining note in the 5th mode of the harmonic major because it is the only option possible.

Summary of Harmonic Major (5th mode)

Defining notes: root, ♭2, M3, ♮6

Non-defining notes: P4, P5, ♭7

As such the mode can be unambiguously defined by a "**6♭9 chord**."

Harmonic Major (♭6th mode)
aka Lydian Augmented ♯2

Root

The root is a defining note by virtue of it being the "home base."

Second

Here, the ♯2 is a defining note by virtue of its establishing that the mode is *"not the 3rd mode of the jazz minor."*

Third

Here, the M3 is a defining note by virtue of its establishing that the mode is *"not minorish."* (Also that the mode is "not a diminished scale minus one note").

Fourth

Here, the ♯4 cannot be lowered, because that creates a chromatic cluster between it and the ♯2 and the M3. Also, the ♯4 cannot be raised, because that creates a chromatic cluster between it and the ♯5 and ♮6.

As such, the ♯4 is a non-defining note because it is the only option possible (in spite of its alteration).

Fifth

Here, the ♯5 is a defining note by virtue of its establishing that the mode is *"not the ♭6th mode of the harmonic minor."*

Sixth

Here, the ♮6 cannot be raised, because that creates a chromatic cluster between it and the ♮7 and the root. Also, the ♮6 cannot be lowered (♭6 = ♯5).

As such, the ♮6 is a non-defining note in the b6th mode of the harmonic major because it is the only option possible.

Seventh

Here, the ♮7 cannot be lowered, because that creates a chromatic cluster between it and the ♯5 and the ♮6.

However, in order to avoid the implication that the mode is the 7th mode of the jazz minor, the ♮7 must be present.

Summary of Harmonic Major (♭6th mode)

Defining notes: root, ♯2, M3, ♯5, ♮7

Non-defining notes: ♯4, ♮6

As such the mode can be unambiguously defined by a "**Maj7♯5♯9 chord**."

Harmonic Major (7th mode) aka Locrian ♭♭7

Root

The root is a defining note by virtue of it being the "home base."

Second

Here, the ♭2 is a defining note by virtue of its establishing that the mode is *"not a diminished scale minus one note."*

Third

Here, the m3 cannot be lowered, because that creates a chromatic cluster between it and the ♭2 and the root.

Also, the m3 cannot be raised, because that creates a chromatic cluster between it and the P4 and the ♭5.

As such, the m3 is a non-defining note because it is the only option possible.

Fourth

Here, the P4 is a defining note by virtue of its establishing that the mode is *"not the 7th mode of the harmonic minor."*

Fifth

Here, the ♭5 cannot be raised, because that creates a chromatic cluster between it and the ♭6 and ♭♭7. Also, the ♭5 cannot be lowered (♭♭5 = P4).

As such, the ♭5 is a non-defining note because it is the only option possible (in spite of its alteration).

Sixth*

Here, the ♭6 cannot be lowered (♭♭6 = ♭5). Also, the ♭6 cannot be raised (♮6 = ♭♭7).

As such, the ♭6 is a non-defining note because it is the only option possible.

Seventh

Here, the ♭♭7 is a defining note by virtue of its establishing that the mode is *"not Locrian."*

*NB. In order to avoid the implication that the mode is the 2nd mode of the jazz minor, the ♭6 must be present.

Summary of Harmonic Major (7th mode)

Defining notes: root, ♭2, P4, ♭6, ♭♭7

Non-defining notes: m3, ♭5

As such the mode can be unambiguously defined by a "**dim11♭9♭13 (no m3, no ♭5) chord.**"

ModeChord Inversions

Out of the 28 possible ModeChords <u>there are **16 unique** ones</u>, plus 12 that are duplicates of some subset.

In the **Ionian** set there are **two** duplicate subsets: **Lydian** and **Mixolydian**

In the **jazz minor** set there are **three**: **Mel b3, Mel 4, Mel 5**

In the **harmonic minor** there are *two* x **two**: *Hm 1 / Hm b3*, and **Hm 2 / Hm 5**

In the **harmonic major** there are **three**: **HM 1, HM 6, HM 7**

This makes several "inversions" possible. Since a majority of these subsets are unlike any others, those chord notes can be voiced any number of ways and *still* continue to identify their specific mode.

The distinctive voicings are capable of establishing the inherent mode, even if the root is not in the bass.

And why is that useful? Because you can make lots more interesting bass lines by moving through inversions other than by root-root-root-root-root-root-root- …

(NB. To avoid ambiguity, bass lines using the "duplicates" should be handled
with care. Should they best have the *root* in the bottom? Or next choice
the *"(usually) non-defining P5"*? 3rd choice – the *3rd*?)

(The **"rooted voicings"** below are only *"suggested voicings"*.
Other options are certainly possible.)

Summary of the C Ionian Set of ModeChords

mode	rooted voicing	alpha order	#
Ionian	C B A E	A B C E	4
Dorian	D C F B E	B C D E F	5
Phrygian	E G C F	C E F G	4
Lydian	**F A B E G**	**A B E F G**	**5**
Mixolydian	**G F A B E**	**A B E F G**	**5**
Aeolian	A C F G B E	A B C E F G	6
Locrian	B F A C G	A B C F G	5

Summary of the C Jazz Minor Set of ModeChords

mode	rooted voicing	alpha order	#
Mel 1	C A E♭ B	A B C E♭	4
Mel 2	D F B E♭	B D E♭ F	4
Mel ♭3	**E♭ G A D F B**	**A B D E♭ F G**	**6**
Mel 4	**F A E♭ G B D**	**A B D E♭ F G**	**6**
Mel 5	**G B E♭ F B D**	**A B D E♭ F G**	**6**
Mel 6	A C F B E♭ G	A B C E♭ F G	6
Mel 7	B E♭ A D G C F	A B C D E♭ F G	7

Summary of the A Harmonic minor Set of ModeChords

mode	rooted voicing	alpha order	#
Hm 1	*A F G♯ C E*	*A C E F G♯*	5
Hm 2	**B F G♯ C E**	**B C E F G♯**	5
Hm ♭3	*C F A B E G♯*	*A C E F G♯*	5
Hm 4	D F G♯ C E	C D E F G♯	5
Hm 5	**E C F G♯ B**	**B C E F G♯**	5
Hm ♭6	F A E G♯	A E F G♯	4
Hm 7	G♯ C F A B E	A B C E F G♯	6

Summary of the C Harmonic Major Set of ModeChords

mode	rooted voicing	alpha order	#
HM 1	**C A♭ B E G**	**A♭ B C E G**	5
HM 2	D F A♭ C E B	A♭ B C D E F	6
HM 3	E A♭ C F G B	A♭ B C E F G	6
HM 4	F C E A♭ B	A♭ B C E F	5
HM 5	G E A♭ B	A♭ B E G	4
HM ♭6	**A♭ C E G B**	**A♭ B C E G**	5
HM 7	B A♭ C E G	A♭ B C E G	5

Descriptive Tetrachord Nomenclature

Tetrachord spanning a minor 3rd

Chromatic Tetrachord
formula:	R-h-h-h
degrees:	1 ♭2 ♭♭3 ♭♭4
example 1:	B♯ C♯ D E♭
example 2:	C D♭ E♭♭ F♭♭

Tetrachords spanning a major 3rd

Diminished ♭♭3 Tetrachord
formula:	R-h-h-W
degrees:	1 ♭2 ♭♭3 ♭4
example 1:	B♯ C♯ D E
example 2:	C D♭ E♭♭ F♭

Diminished Tetrachord
formula:	R-h-W-h
degrees:	1 ♭2 ♭3 ♭4
example 1:	B♯ C♯ D♯ E
example 2:	C D♭ E♭ F♭

Diminished ♮2 Tetrachord
formula:	R-W-h-h
degrees:	1 2 ♭3 ♭4
example 1:	B♯ Cx D♯ E
example 2:	C D E♭ F♭

Diatonic Tetrachords spanning a perfect 4th

Major Tetrachord
formula:	R-W-W-h
degrees:	1 2 3 4
example:	C D E F

Minor Tetrachord
formula:	R-W-h-W
degrees:	1 2 ♭3 4
example:	C D E♭ F

Phrygian Tetrachord
formula:	R-h-W-W
degrees:	1 ♭2 ♭3 4
example:	C D♭ E♭ F

Tetrachords spanning a perfect 4th
(incorporating an augmented second)

Phrygian ♭♭3 Tetrachord
formula:	R-h-h-♯2
degrees:	1 ♭2 ♭♭3 4
example 1:	C D♭ E♭♭ F
example 2:	C C♯ D F

Harmonic Tetrachord
formula:	R-h-♯2-h
degrees:	1 b2 3 4
example:	C D♭ E F

Major ♯2 Tetrachord
formula:	R-♯2-h-h
degrees:	1 ♯2 3 4
example:	C D♯ E F

Diatonic Tetrachord spanning a tritone

Lydian Tetrachord
formula:	R-W-W-W
degrees:	1 2 3 ♯4
example:	C D E F♯

Tetrachords spanning a tritone
(incoporating an augmented second)

Phrygian ♯4 Tetrachord
formula:	R-h-W-♯2
degrees:	1 ♭2 ♭3 ♯4
example:	C D♭ E♭ F♯

Minor ♯4 Tetrachord
formula:	R-W-h-♯2
degrees:	1 2 ♭3 ♯4
example:	C D E♭ F♯

Lydian ♯3 Tetrachord
formula:	R-W-♯2-h
degrees:	1 2 ♯3 ♯4
example:	C D E♯ F♯

Descriptive Tetrachord Nomenclature (cont'd)

Tetrachords spanning a tritone (incorporating an augmented second) (continued)	Tetrachords spanning a tritone (incorporating a double-sharped second aka major third)
Lydian ♭2 Tetrachord formula: R-h-♯2-W degrees: 1 ♭2 3 ♯4 example: C D♭ E F♯	Messiaen 5 Tetrachord formula: R-h-h-x2(M3) degrees: 1 ♭2 ♭♭3 ♯4 example: C D♭ E♭♭ F♯
Lydian ♯2 Tetrachord formula: R-♯2-h-W degrees: 1 ♯2 3 ♯4 example: C D♯ E F♯	Super Harmonic Tetrachord formula: R-h-x2(M3)-h degrees: 1 ♭2 ♯3 ♯4 example: C D♭ E♯ F♯
Blues Diminished Tetrachord formula: R-♯2-W-h degrees: 1 ♯2 ♯3 ♯4 example: C D♯ E♯ F♯ degrees: 1 ♭3 4 ♭5 example: C E♭ F G♭	Messiaen inverse 5 Tetrachord formula: R-x2(M3)-h-h degrees: 1 x2 ♯3 ♯4 example: C Dx E♯ F♯

Descriptive Octatonic Scale Nomenclature

A "bebop scale" is *a common heptatonic scale with an added note."*

The octatonic scales below are all common heptatonic scales with an "added note."

In the case of the modes of the Bebop Dominant Scale, they all consist of a hybrid of two of the Greek modes. On page 196, each scale in this set has been described by placing the predominating greek mode as the initial element of the 8-note mode's hybrid name.

Every one of these octatonic scales can also be descriptively described as

[*common scale*] **add** [*extra note*]

However, this type of moniker can be deceiving as to <u>function</u>, as in the case of a Dorian mode with an added major third *"Dorian add ♮3"* (bebop dorian / bebop minor) which may function as a *"Mixolydian add ♭3"* (Mixodorian).

Definitions:

ultra-	includes ♮7
dominant	includes ♮3 & ♭7
augmented	includes #5
quintal	includes P5
blues	includes ♭5
lydian	includes #4
quartal	includes P4
super	includes ♭4
major	includes ♮3
minor	includes ♭3
infra-	includes ♭2

Certain scales are identified by their tetrachords as well.

Example:
B Diminished-WholeTone scale
(aka dim-WT, Superlocrian, altered scale)

This scale consists of a diminished tetrachord on the bottom and
a wholetone (Lydian) tetrachord on the top:

| B diminished tetrachord | F Lydian tetrachord |

A number of these octatonic scales are used around the world. Where known, their alternate names are listed.

The two most popular sets of "bebop scales" are the modes of the "type one radially symmetrical" bebop major scale and the "type 2 rs" bebop dominant scale.

Modes of the C Bebop Major Scale

(axes of type one radial symmetry = <u>D</u> and <u>A</u>♭)

1st mode

name:	**C Bebop Major Scale**
desc:	Ionian add ♭6
scale:	C D E F G A♭ A B C
formula:	R-W-W-h-W-h-h-W-h
degrees:	1 2 3 4 5 ♭6 6 7 8
usage:	over major quality chords

2nd mode

name:	**D Dorian Blues Scale**
desc:	Dorian add ♭5
scale:	D E F G A♭ A B C D
formula:	R-W-h-W-h-h-W-h-W
degrees:	1 2 ♭3 4 ♭5 5 6 ♭7 8
usage:	over Dorian minor chords & blues 7th chords

3rd mode

name:	**E Spanish Phrygian Scale**
desc:	hybrid–Phrygian & Phrygian dominant
scale:	E F G G♯ A B C D E
formula:	R-h-W-h-h-W-h-W-W
degrees:	1 ♭2 ♭3 3 4 5 ♭6 ♭7 8
usage:	in phrygian environments and V7 of composite minor

4th mode

name:	**F Lydian Minor Octatonic**
desc:	Lydian add ♭3
scale:	F G A♭ A B C D E F
formula:	R-W-h-h-W-h-W-W-h
degrees:	1 2 ♭3 3 ♯4 5 6 7 8
usage:	over major quality chords

5th mode

name:	**G Infra-Mixolydian Octatonic**
desc:	Mixolydian add ♭9
scale:	G A♭ A B C D E F G
formula:	R-h-h-W-h-W-W-h-W
degrees:	1 ♭2 2 3 4 5 6 ♭7 8
usage:	over 7♭9 chords

♭6th mode

name:	**G♯ Diminished Augmented Octatonic** (aka augmented diminished, Lyxian)
desc:	I G♯dim tetrachord I D I Edim tetrachord I
scale:	I G♯ A B C I D I E F G A♭ I
formula:	R-h-W-h-W-W-h-W-h
degrees:	1 ♭2 ♭3 ♭4 ♭5 ♭6 6 7 8
usage:	w/ diminished & augmented quality chords

6th mode

name:	**A Bebop Harmonic Minor Scale** (aka Bebop Natural Minor, Ultra-Aeolian, Maqam Nahawand, Raga Suha, Suha Kanada)
desc:	hybrid – harmonic minor & Aeolian
scale:	A B C D E F G G♯ A
formula:	R-W-h-W-W-h-W-h-h
degrees:	1 2 ♭3 4 5 ♭6 ♭7 7 8
usage:	over (aeolian) minor quality chords

7th mode

name:	**B Locrian Diminished Octatonic**
desc:	Locrian add ♮6
scale:	B C D E F G A♭ A B
formula:	R-h-W-W-h-W-h-h-W
degrees:	1 ♭2 ♭3 4 ♭5 ♭6 ♭♭7 ♭7 8
usage:	over half-diminished chords & diminished 7th chords

Modes of the G Bebop Dominant Scale

(axes of type two radial symmetry = <u>F/F♯</u> and <u>B/C</u>)

4th mode

name:	C Lydionian
	(aka *Ichikotsucho, Raga Yaman Kalyan, Chaya Nat, Bihag, Hamir Kalyani, Kedar, Genus Diatonicum Veterum Correctum, Gaud Sarang, Gregorian nr.5, Kubilai's Mongol scale*)
desc:	hybrid – Lydian & Ionian (Lydian add P4 or Ionian add ♯4)
scale:	C D E F F♯ G A B C
formula:	R-W-W-h-h-h-W-W-h
degrees:	1 2 3 4 ♯4 5 6 7 8
usage:	over major quality chords

5th mode

name:	**D Mixodorian**
	(aka *Bebop Dorian, Bebop Minor, Raga Zilla*)
desc:	hybrid – Mixolydian & Dorian (Mixolydian add ♭3 or Dorian add ♮3)
scale:	D E F F♯ G A B C D
formula:	R-W-h-h-h-W-W-h-W
degrees:	1 2 ♭3 3 4 5 6 ♭7 8
usage:	over dominant quality and secondary dominant chords

6th mode

name:	**E Phrygiolian**
desc:	hybrid – Phrygian & Aeolian (Phrygian add ♮2, Aeolian add ♭2, infra-Aeolian)
scale:	E F F♯ G A B C D E
formula:	R-h-h-h-W-W-h-W-W
degrees:	1 ♭2 2 ♭3 4 5 ♭6 ♭7 8
usage:	???

♭7th mode

name:	**F Lydiocrian**
desc:	hybrid – Lydian & Locrian (Lydian add ♭2, infra-Lydian)
scale:	F F♯ G A B C D E F
formula:	R-h-h-W-W-h-W-W-h
degrees:	1 ♭2 2 3 ♯4 5 6 7 8
usage:	???

7th mode

name:	**F♯ Locrydian**
desc:	hybrid – Locrian & Lydian (Locrian add ♮7, Ultra-locrian)
scale:	F♯ G A B C D E F F♯
formula:	R-h-W-W-h-W-W-h-h
degrees:	1 ♭2 ♭3 4 ♭5 ♭6 ♭7 7 8
usage:	over half-diminished chords, altered 7ths

1st mode

name:	**G Mixionian**
	(aka *Ultra-Mixolydian, Bebop Dominant Scale, Genus Diatonicum, Raga Khamaj, Desh Malhar, Alhaiya Bilaval, Devagandhari, Maqam Shawq Awir, Gregorian nr.6, Chinese Eight-Tone*)
desc:	hybrid – Mixolydian & Ionian (Mixolydian add ♮7 or Ionian add ♭7)
scale:	G A B C D E F F♯ G
formula:	R-W-W-h-W-W-h-h-h
degrees:	1 2 3 4 5 6 ♭7 7 8
usage:	over dominant quality chords

2nd mode

name:	**A Doriolian**
	(aka *Raga Mukhari, Anandabhairavi Deshi, Manji, Gregorian nr.1*)
desc:	hybrid – Dorian & Aeolian (Dorian add ♭6 or Aeolian add ♮6)
scale:	A B C D E F F♯ G A
formula:	R-W-h-W-W-h-h-h-W
degrees:	1 2 ♭3 4 5 ♭6 6 ♭7 8
usage:	over (Dorian) minor chords

3rd mode

name:	**B Phrygiolocrian**
desc:	hybrid – Phrygian & Locrian (Phrygian add ♭5 or Locrian add P5)
scale:	B C D E F F♯ G A B
formula:	R-h-W-W-h-h-h-W-W
degrees:	1 ♭2 ♭3 4 ♭5 5 ♭6 ♭7 8
usage:	over ♭2 minor chords and altered minor chords (m7♭5, m7♭9♭5)

Modes of the C Ionian Minor Octatonic Scale

(non-symmetrical)

1st mode

name:	**C Ionian Minor Octatonic**
desc:	hybrid – Ionian and jazz minor (Ionian add ♭3 or jazz minor add ♮3)
scale:	C D E♭ E F G A B C
formula:	R-W-h-h-h-W-W-W-h
degrees:	1 2 ♭3 3 4 5 6 7 8
usage:	over major quality chords

2nd mode

name:	**D Double Dorian Octatonic** (aka *Infra-Dorian, Adonai Malakh*)
desc:	hybrid – Dorian ♭2 & Dorian (Dorian add ♭2)
scale:	D E♭ E F G A B C D
formula:	R-h-h-h-W-W-W-h-W
degrees:	1 ♭2 2 ♭3 4 5 6 ♭7 8
usage:	Jewish

♭3rd mode

name:	**E♭ Infra-Lydian Augmented Octatonic**
desc:	Lydian augmented add ♭9
scale:	E♭ E F G A B C D E♭
formula:	R-h-h-W-W-W-h-W-h
degrees:	1 ♭2 2 3 ♯4 ♯5 6 7 8
usage:	???

3rd mode

name:	**E Ultra-Phrygian Octatonic**
desc:	Phrygian add ♮7
scale:	E F G A B C D D♯ E
formula:	R-h-W-W-W-h-W-h-h
degrees:	1 ♭2 ♭3 4 5 ♭6 ♭7 7 8
usage:	Phrygian

4th mode

name:	**F Bebop Lydian Dominant Scale**
desc:	hybrid – Lydian dominant & Lydian (Lydian dominant add ♮7 or Lydian add ♭7)
scale:	F G A B C D E♭ E F
formula:	R-W-W-W-h-W-h-h-h
degrees:	1 2 3 ♯4 5 6 ♭7 7 8
usage:	over dominant quality chords

5th mode

name:	**G Mixolydian Augmented Octatonic** (aka *Dominant Augmented, Dogmented*)
desc:	hybrid – Mixolydian ♭6 & Mixolydian (Mixolydian add ♯5)
scale:	G A B C D D♯ E F G
formula:	R-W-W-h-W-h-h-h-W
degrees:	1 2 3 4 5 ♯5 6 ♭7 8
usage:	over 7♯5 chords

6th mode

name:	**A Aeolian Blues Scale**
desc:	hybrid – Aeolian & Aeolian ♭5/Locrian ♮2 (Aeolian add ♭5 or Aeolian ♭5 add P5 or Locrian ♮2 add P5)
scale:	A B C D E♭ E F G A
formula:	R-W-h-W-h-h-h-W-W
degrees:	1 2 ♭3 4 ♭5 5 ♭6 ♭7 8
usage:	over minor blues

7th mode

name:	**B Altered Quartal Octatonic** (aka *Eight-Tone Spanish, Espla's Scale*)
desc:	hybrid – superlocrian & Locrian (altered scale add P4 or Locrian add dim4)
scale:	B C D E♭ E F G A B
formula:	R-h-W-h-h-h-W-W-W
degrees:	1 ♭2 ♭3 ♭4 4 ♭5 ♭6 ♭7 8
usage:	over Alt7, 7sus, Spanish

Modes of the C Infra-Ionian Octatonic Scale

(non-symmetrical)

1st mode

name:	**C Infra-Ionian Octatonic**
desc:	Ionian add ♭9
scale:	C D♭ D E F G A B C
formula:	R-h-h-W-h-W-W-W-h
degrees:	1 ♭2 2 3 4 5 6 7 8
usage:	???

b2nd mode

name:	**C♯ Ultra-Superlocrian Octatonic**
desc:	Superlocrian add ♮7
scale:	C♯ D E F G A B C C♯
formula:	R-h-W-h-W-W-W-h-h
degrees:	1 ♭2 ♭3 ♭4 ♭5 ♭6 ♭7 7 8
usage:	over altered 7th chords

2nd mode

name:	**D Ultra-Dorian Octatonic**
	(aka *Raga Mian Ki Malhar*)
desc:	hybrid - Dorian & jazz minor
	(Dorian add ♮7 or jazz minor add ♭7)
scale:	D E F G A B C C♯ D
formula:	R-W-h-W-W-W-h-h-h
degrees:	1 2 ♭3 4 5 6 ♭7 7 8
usage:	over (Dorian) minor chords

3rd mode

name:	**E Double Phrygian Octatonic**
desc:	hybrid - Phrygian & Phrygian ♮6/Dorian ♭2
	(Phrygian ♮6 add ♭6 or Phrygian add ♮6 or
	Dorian ♭2 add ♭6)
scale:	E F G A B C C♯ D E
formula:	R-h-W-W-W-h-h-h-W
degrees:	1 ♭2 ♭3 4 5 ♭6 6 ♭7 8
usage:	Phrygian

4th mode

name:	**F Lydydian Augmented Octatonic**
desc:	hybrid – Lydian & Lydian augmented
	(Lydian add ♯5 or Lydian aug. add P5)
scale:	F G A B C C♯ D E F
formula:	R-W-W-W-h-h-h-W-h
degrees:	1 2 3 ♯4 5 ♯5 6 7 8
usage:	???

5th mode

name:	**G Mixolydian Blues Scale**
desc:	hybrid – Mixolydian & Lydian dominant
	(Mixolydian add ♭5 or Lydian dom. add P4)
scale:	G A B C D♭ D E F G
formula:	R-W-W-h-h-h-W-h-W
degrees:	1 2 3 4 ♭5 5 6 ♭7 8
usage:	over blues 7ths

6th mode

name:	**A Jazz Mixolydian Minor Octatonic**
desc:	hybrid – jazz Mixolydian & Aeolian
	(jazz Mixolydian add ♭3 or Aeolian add ♮3)
scale:	A B C C♯ D E F G A
formula:	R-W-h-h-h-W-h-W-W
degrees:	1 2 ♭3 3 4 5 ♭6 ♭7 8
usage:	???

7th mode

name:	**B Double Locrian Octatonic**
desc:	hybrid – Locrian & Locrian ♮2
	(Locrian add ♮2 or Locrian ♮2 add ♭2)
scale:	B C C♯ D E F G A B
formula:	R-h-h-h-W-h-W-W-W
degrees:	1 ♭2 2 ♭3 4 ♭5 ♭6 ♭7 8
usage:	???

Modes of the C Bebop Melodic Minor Scale

(non-symmetrical)

1st mode
name: **C Bebop Melodic Minor Scale**
(aka *Zirafkend*)
desc: jazz minor add ♭6 or
harmonic minor add ♮6
scale: C D E♭ F G A♭ A B C
formula: R-W-h-W-W-h-h-W-h
degrees: 1 2 ♭3 4 5 ♭6 6 ♮7 8
usage: over (Dorian) minor chords

2nd mode
name: **D Jazz Phrygian Blues Octatonic**
desc: Phyrgian ♮6 add ♭5, jazz Phrygian add ♭5
or Dorian ♭2 add ♯4
scale: D E♭ F G A♭ A B C D
formula: R-h-W-W-h-h-W-h-W
degrees: 1 ♭2 ♭3 4 ♯4 5 6 ♭7 8
usage: over diminished chords

♭3rd mode
name: **E♭ Major Minor Octatonic**
desc: tetrachords: | E♭ major | A minor |
Lydian augmented add P4
scale: | E♭ F G A♭ | A B C D | E♭
formula: R-W-W-h-h-W-h-W-h
degrees: 1 2 3 4 ♯4 ♯5 6 ♮7 8
usage: ???

4th mode
name: **F Lydian Dominant Minor Octatonic**
desc: Lydian dominant add ♭3
scale: F G A♭ A B C D E♭ F
formula: R-W-h-h-W-h-W-h-W
degrees: 1 2 ♭3 3 ♯4 5 6 ♭7 8
usage: over dominant chords

5th mode
name: **G Infra-Jazz Mixolydian Octatonic**
desc: jazz Mixolydian add ♭9 or
Phrygian Dominant add ♮2
scale: G A♭ A B C D E♭ F G
formula: R-h-h-W-h-W-h-W-W
degrees: 1 ♭2 2 3 4 5 ♭6 ♭7 8
usage: over 7♭9

♯5th mode
name: **G♯ Ultra-Diminished Octatonic**
desc: hW-diminished ♮7
scale: | G♯ A B C | D | E♭ F G A♭ |
formula: R-h-W-h-W-h-W-W-h
degrees: 1 ♭2 ♭3 ♭4 ♭5 5 6 ♮7 8
usage: ???

6th mode
name: **A Ultra-Aeolian Diminished Octatonic**
desc: Aeolian ♭5 add ♮7, Aeolian diminished add ♮7
or Locrian ♮2 add ♮7
scale: A B C D E♭ F G A♭ A
formula: R-W-h-W-h-W-W-h-h
degrees: 1 2 ♭3 4 ♭5 ♭6 ♭7 ♮7 8
usage: over altered minor chords

7th mode
name: **B Altered Diminished Octatonic**
desc: Superlocrian add ♮6
scale: B C D E♭ F G A♭ A B
formula: R-h-W-h-W-W-h-h-W
degrees: 1 ♭2 ♭3 ♭4 ♭5 ♭6 ♭♭7 ♭7 8
usage: over half-diminished, diminished and
alt7 chords

Modes of the C Jazz Minor Blues Scale

(non-symmetrical)

1st mode
name: **C Jazz Minor Blues Scale**
desc: jazz minor add ♭5
scale: C D E♭ F G♭ G A B C
formula: R-W-h-W-h-h-W-W-h
degrees: 1 2 ♭3 4 ♭5 5 6 ♮7 8
usage: over (Dorian) minor chords

2nd mode
name: **D Super-Jazz Phrygian Octatonic**
desc: Phrygian ♮6 add ♭4, jazz Phrygian add ♭4
Dorian ♭2 add ♭4
scale: | D E♭ F F♯ | G A B C | D
formula: R-h-W-h-h-W-W-h-W
degrees: 1 ♭2 ♭3 3 4 5 6 ♭7 8
usage: over 7♭9 chords

♭3rd mode
name: **E♭ Lydian Augmented Minor Octatonic**
desc: Lydian augmented add ♭3
scale: E♭ F G♭ G A B C D E♭
formula: R-W-h-h-W-W-h-W-h
degrees: 1 2 ♭3 3 ♯4 ♯5 6 ♭7 8
usage: ???

4th mode
name: **F Infra-Lydian Dominant**
desc: Lydian dominant add ♭9
scale: F G♭ G A B C D E♭ F
formula: R-h-h-W-W-h-W-h-W
degrees: 1 b2 2 3 ♯4 5 6 ♭7 8
usage: over 7♭9 chords

♯4th mode
name: **F♯ Locrydian ♭♭7 Scale**
desc: tetrachords: | F♯ Phrygian | C minor |
scale: | F♯ G A B | C D E♭ F | F♯
formula: R-h-W-W-h-W-h-W-h
degrees: 1 ♭2 ♭3 4 ♭5 ♭6 ♭♭7 ♮7 8
usage: over half-diminished and
diminished chords

5th mode
name: **G Ultra-Jazz Mixolydian Octatonic**
desc: jazz Mixolydian add ♮7 or
harmonic major add ♭7
scale: G A B C D E♭ F F♯ G
formula: R-W-W-h-W-h-W-h-h
degrees: 1 2 3 4 5 ♭6 ♭7 ♮7 8
usage: over 7♯5 chords

6th mode
name: **A Wh-Diminished ♭7 Octatonic**
desc: Wh-diminished ♭7
Aeolian ♭5 add ♮6 or Locrian ♮2 add ♮6
scale: A B C D E♭ F F♯ G A
formula: R-W-h-W-h-W-h-h-W
degrees: 1 2 ♭3 4 ♭5 ♭6 6 ♭7 8
usage: over diminished & half-diminished chords

7th mode
name: **B Altered Quintal Octatonic**
desc: Superlocrian add P5
scale: B C D E♭ F F♯ G A B
formula: R-h-W-h-W-h-h-W-W
degrees: 1 ♭2 ♭3 ♭4 ♭5 5 ♭6 ♭7 8
usage: over alt7 chords

Modes of the C Lydian Chromatic Octatonic Scale

(axes of type one radial symmetry = <u>D</u> and <u>A♭</u>)

1st mode

name:	**C Lydian Chromatic Octatonic 1**
	(aka Lydian dominant augmented, Lydian dogmented)
desc:	tetrachords:	C Lydian	G chromatic	Lydian dominant add ♯5
scale:		C D E F♯	G A♭ A B♭	C
formula:	R-W-W-W-h-h-h-h-W
degrees:	1 2 3 ♯4 5 ♯5 6 ♭7 8
usage:	over 7♭5 and 7♯5

2nd mode

name:	**D Jazz Mixolydian Blues Scale**
desc:	jazz Mixolydian add ♭5
scale:	D E F♯ G A♭ A B♭ C D
formula:	R-W-W-h-h-h-h-W-W
degrees:	1 2 3 4 ♭5 5 ♭6 ♭7 8
usage:	over 7♭5 and 7♯5

3rd mode

name:	**E Whole-Tone Minor Quartal Octatonic**
desc:	whole-tone scale add ♭3 and P4
	Locrian ♮2 add ♮3 / Aeolian ♭5 add ♮3
scale:	E F♯ G G♯ A B♭ C D E
formula:	R-W-h-h-h-h-W-W-W
degrees:	1 2 ♭3 3 4 ♭5 ♭6 ♭7 8
usage:	over 7♭5 and 7♯5

4th mode

name:	**F♯ Chromatic Lydian Octatonic 1**
desc:	tetrachords:	F♯ chromatic	B♭ Lydian	Superlocrian add ♮2
scale:		F♯ G A♭ A	B♭ C D E	F♯
formula:	R-h-h-h-h-W-W-W-W
degrees:	1 ♭2 2 ♭3 ♭4 ♭5 ♭6 ♭7 8
usage:	over 7♭5 and 7♯5 and half-diminished 7

5th mode

name:	**G Chromatic Lydian Octatonic 2**
desc:	tetrachords:	G chromatic	C Lydian	jazz minor add ♭9, infra-jazz minor
scale:		G A♭ A B♭	C D E F♯	G
formula:	R-h-h-h-W-W-W-W-h
degrees:	1 ♭2 2 ♭3 4 5 6 ♮7 8
usage:	???

♭6th mode

name:	**G♯ Infra-Ultra Whole-Tone Octatonic**
desc:	whole-tone scale add ♭2 and ♮7
scale:	G♯ A B♭ C D E F♯ G G♯
formula:	R-h-h-W-W-W-W-h-h
degrees:	1 ♭2 2 3 ♭5 ♭6 ♭7 ♮7 8
usage:	over 7♭5♭9 and 7♯5♭9

6th mode

name:	**A Ultra-Jazz Phrygian Octatonic**
desc:	Phrygian ♮6 add ♮7 / Dorian ♭2 add ♮7
scale:	A B♭ C D E F♯ G G♯ A
formula:	R-h-W-W-W-W-h-h-h
degrees:	1 ♭2 ♭3 4 5 6 ♭7 ♮7 8
usage:	???

7th mode

name:	**B♭ Lydian Chromatic Octatonic 2**
desc:	tetrachords:	B♭ Lydian	F♯ chromatic	Lydian augmented add ♭7
scale:		B♭ C D E	F♯ G A♭ A	B♭
formula:	R-W-W-W-W-h-h-h-h
degrees:	1 2 3 ♯4 ♯5 6 ♭7 ♮7 8
usage:	over 7♭5 and 7♯5

199

Quartals

Quartals are structures built by stacking consecutive 4ths.

These 4ths can be:

Perfect 4th (P4 = 5 half-steps)

Augmented 4th (aka "♯4", "tritone", "t" = 6 half-steps)

Diminished 4th (aka "♭4", "dim4", "d" = 4 half-steps)

In the ionian set of modes, only P4s and one ♯4 exist.

In the jazz minor, harmonic minor and harmonic major (and their modes), diminished 4ths also exist.

Quartals are most typically used either as bottom-up harmonic structures or as top-down non-functional harmonizations of melody notes.

The smallest quartal structure contains a minimum of 3 notes,
but quartals *can* contain more than three.

In the case of a 3-note harmonic structure consisting solely of P4s built from the bottom upwards, the designation "**Q**" is used here.

Example: CQ = C F B♭

In the case of a 3-note bottom-up harmonic structure which contains an interval that is an altered 4th, the designations "**t**" (for tritone) and "**d**" (for diminished 4th) are used here.

Examples:

CQt = C F B

FtQ = F B E

BQd = B E A♭

BdQ = B E♭ A♭

In cases where no P4 is present in the structure, conventional tertian terminology is used.

Examples:

F B E♭ = F7♭5 (no 3)

B E♭ A = B7 (no 5)

In the case of a 3-note top-down non-functional melodic harmonization consisting of solely P4s, a lower case "**q**" is used.

Example: B♭q = B♭ F C (spelled from top to bottom)

As above, in the case of a 3-note top-down non-functional melodic harmonization structure which contains an interval that is an altered 4th, the designations "**t**" (for tritone) and "**d**" (for diminished 4th) are used.

Examples:

Gqt = G D A♭ (spelled from top to bottom)

Btq = B F C (spelled from top to bottom)

A♭qd = A♭ E♭ B (spelled from top to bottom)

A♭dq = A♭ E B (spelled from top to bottom)

In the case of a 4-note harmonic structure consisting solely of three P4s stacked from the bottom upwards, the designation "Q3" is used.

Example: CQ3 (= CQQQ) = C F B♭ E♭

In the case of a 4-note top-down non-functional melodic harmonization consisting of solely P4s, "**q3**" is used.

Example: E♭q3 = E♭ B♭ F C (spelled from top to bottom)

(NB. Inversions of quartals can easily be represented by slash chords.
Examples: FtQ/B, FtQ/E, CQt/F, CQt/B, etc.)

In the cases of 4-note (or more) quartals containing both P4s and Altered 4ths,
the intervals are simply listed in order
(NB. FtQ2 = FtQQ, Btq2 = Btqq)

Bottom-Up examples	Top-Down examples (spelled from top to bottom)
CQtQ = C F B E	Eqtq = E B F C
FtQ2 = F B E A	Btq2 = B F C G
GQ2t = G C F B	Aq2t = A E B F
CQtd = C F B E♭	Dqtd = D A E♭ B
BQdt = B E A♭ D	A♭qdt = A♭ E♭ B F
BdtQ = B E♭ A D	E♭dtq = E♭ B F C
FtdQ = F B E♭ A♭	Dtdq = D A♭ E B
BdQt = B E♭ A♭ D	A♭dqt = A♭ E B F
FtQd = F B E A♭	Dtqd = D A♭ E♭ B

3-note and 4-note Quartal Studies
in the four most common heptatonic sets

Ionian Quartals						
C F B	CQt	Btq		C F B E	CQtQ	Eqtq
D G C	DQ	Cq		D G C F	DQ3	Fq3
E A D	EQ	Dq		E A D G	EQ3	Gq3
F B E	FtQ	Eqt		F B E A	FtQ2	Aq2t
G C F	GQ	Fq		G C F B	GQ2t	Btq2
A D G	AQ	Gq		A D G C	AQ3	Cq3
B E A	BQ	Aq		B E A D	BQ3	Dq3

Jazz Minor Quartals

C F B	CQt	Btq	C F B E♭	CQtd	E♭dtq
D G C	DQ	Cq	D G C F	DQ3	Fq3
E♭ A D	E♭tQ	Dqt	E♭ A D G	E♭tQ2	Gq2t
F B E♭	F7♭5 (no 3)		F B E♭ A	F7♭5	
G C F	GQ	Fq	G C F B	GQ2t	Btq2
A D G	AQ	Gq	A D G C	AQ3	Cq3
B E♭ A	B7 (no 5)		B E♭ A D	BdtQ	Dqtd

Harmonic Minor Quartals

C F B	CQt	Btq	C F B E♭	CQtd	E♭dtq
D G C	DQ	Cq	D G C F	DQ3	Fq3
E♭ A♭ D	E♭Qt	Dtq	E♭ A♭ D G	E♭QtQ	Gqtq
F B E♭	F7♭5 (no 3)		F B E♭ A♭	FtdQ	A♭qdt
G C F	GQ	Fq	G C F B	GQ2t	Btq2
A♭ D G	A♭tQ	Gqt	A♭ D G C	A♭tQ2	Cq2t
B E♭ A♭	BdQ	A♭qd	B E♭ A♭ D	BdQt	Dtqd

Harmonic Major Quartals

C F B	CQt	Btq	C F B E	CQtQ	Eqtq
D G C	DQ	Cq	D G C F	DQ3	Fq3
E A♭ D	E7 (no 5)		E A♭ D G	EdtQ	Gqtd
F B E	FtQ	Eqt	F B E A♭	FtQd	A♭dqt
G C F	GQ	Fq	G C F B	GQ2t	Btq2
A♭ D G	A♭tQ	Gqt	A♭ D G C	A♭tQ2	Cq2t
B E A♭	BQd	A♭dq	B E A♭ D	BQdt	Dtdq

3-note P4 Quartal Permutations over ii-V7-I Progressions (using the Ionian set)

♭3 = min 3rd interval above root
♭7 = min 7th interval above root
7 = Maj 7th interval above root

Minor quality voicings:		Dominant 7 quality voicings:	
1 11 ♭7	(m11)	9 5 1	(9th)
9 5 1	(m9)	3 6 9	(13th)
11 ♭7 ♭3	(m11)	6 9 5	(13th)
5 8 11	(m11)		
6 9 5	(m13)		

Major quality voicings:	
9 5 1	(Maj9)
3 6 9	(Maj69)
6 9 5	(Maj69)
7 3 6	(Maj13no11)

Dmin	1 11 ♭7 (D G C)	**DQ**	descend		Dmin	1 11 ♭7 (D G C)	**DQ**	descend
G7	9 5 1 (A D G)	**AQ**	ascend		G7	3 6 9 (B E A)	**BQ**	descend
Cmaj	9 5 1 (D G C)	**DQ**			Cmaj	6 9 5 (A D G)	**AQ**	
Dmin	1 11 ♭7 (D G C)	**DQ**	descend		Dmin	1 11 ♭7 (D G C)	**DQ**	descend
G7	9 5 1 (A D G)	**AQ**	descend		G7	3 6 9 (B E A)	**BQ**	same
Cmaj	3 6 9 (E A D)	**EQ**			Cmaj	7 3 6 (B E A)	**BQ**	
Dmin	1 11 ♭7 (D G C)	**DQ**	descend		* * * * * * * * * * * * * * * * * *			
G7	9 5 1 (A D G)	**AQ**	same					
Cmaj	6 9 5 (A D G)	**AQ**			Dmin	1 11 ♭7 (D G C)	**DQ**	ascend
					G7	6 9 5 (E A D)	**EQ**	descend
Dmin	1 11 ♭7 (D G C)	**DQ**	descend		Cmaj	9 5 1 (D G C)	**DQ**	
G7	9 5 1 (A D G)	**AQ**	ascend					
Cmaj	7 3 6 (B E A)	**BQ**			Dmin	1 11 ♭7 (D G C)	**DQ**	ascend
					G7	6 9 5 (E A D)	**EQ**	same
* * * * * * * * * * * * * * * * * *					Cmaj	3 6 9 (E A D)	**EQ**	
Dmin	1 11 ♭7 (D G C)	**DQ**	descend		Dmin	1 11 ♭7 (D G C)	**DQ**	ascend
G7	3 6 9 (B E A)	**BQ**	ascend		G7	6 9 5 (E A D)	**EQ**	ascend
Cmaj	9 5 1 (D G C)	**DQ**			Cmaj	6 9 5 (A D G)	**AQ**	
Dmin	1 11 ♭7 (D G C)	**DQ**	descend		Dmin	1 11 ♭7 (D G C)	**DQ**	ascend
G7	3 6 9 (B E A)	**BQ**	ascend		G7	6 9 5 (E A D)	**EQ**	descend
Cmaj	3 6 9 (E A D)	**EQ**			Cmaj	7 3 6 (B E A)	**BQ**	

* * * * * * * * * * * * * * * * * *

Dmin	9 5 1 (E A D)	**EQ**	ascend		Dm	11 ♭7 ♭3 (G C F)	**GQ**	ascend
G7	9 5 1 (A D G)	**AQ**	ascend		G7	9 5 1 (A D G)	**AQ**	ascend
Cmaj	9 5 1 (D G C)	**DQ**			Cmaj	9 5 1 (D G C)	**DQ**	

Dmin	9 5 1 (E A D)	**EQ**	ascend		Dm	11 ♭7 ♭3 (G C F)	**GQ**	ascend
G7	9 5 1 (A D G)	**AQ**	descend		G7	9 5 1 (A D G)	**AQ**	descend
Cmaj	3 6 9 (E A D)	**EQ**			Cmaj	3 6 9 (E A D)	**EQ**	

Dmin	9 5 1 (E A D)	**EQ**	ascend		Dm	11 ♭7 ♭3 (G C F)	**GQ**	ascend
G7	9 5 1 (A D G)	**AQ**	same		G7	9 5 1 (A D G)	**AQ**	same
Cmaj	6 9 5 (A D G)	**AQ**			Cmaj	6 9 5 (A D G)	**AQ**	

Dmin	9 5 1 (E A D)	**EQ**	ascend		Dm	11 ♭7 ♭3 (G C F)	**GQ**	ascend
G7	9 5 1 (A D G)	**AQ**	ascend		G7	9 5 1 (A D G)	**AQ**	ascend
Cmaj	7 3 6 (B E A)	**BQ**			Cmaj	7 3 6 (B E A)	**BQ**	

* * * * * * * * * * * * * * *   * * * * * * * * * * * * * * * *

Dmin	9 5 1 (E A D)	**EQ**	descend		Dm	11 ♭7 ♭3 (G C F)	**GQ**	ascend
G7	3 6 9 (B E A)	**BQ**	ascend		G7	3 6 9 (B E A)	**BQ**	ascend
Cmaj	9 5 1 (D G C)	**DQ**			Cmaj	9 5 1 (D G C)	**DQ**	

Dmin	9 5 1 (E A D)	**EQ**	descend		Dm	11 ♭7 ♭3 (G C F)	**GQ**	ascend
G7	3 6 9 (B E A)	**BQ**	ascend		G7	3 6 9 (B E A)	**BQ**	ascend
Cmaj	3 6 9 (E A D)	**EQ**			Cmaj	3 6 9 (E A D)	**EQ**	

Dmin	9 5 1 (E A D)	**EQ**	descend		Dm	11 ♭7 ♭3 (G C F)	**GQ**	ascend
G7	3 6 9 (B E A)	**BQ**	descend		G7	3 6 9 (B E A)	**BQ**	descend
Cmaj	6 9 5 (A D G)	**AQ**			Cmaj	6 9 5 (A D G)	**AQ**	

Dmin	9 5 1 (E A D)	**EQ**	descend		Dm	11 ♭7 ♭3 (G C F)	**GQ**	ascend
G7	3 6 9 (B E A)	**BQ**	same		G7	3 6 9 (B E A)	**BQ**	same
Cmaj	7 3 6 (B E A)	**BQ**			Cmaj	7 3 6 (B E A)	**BQ**	

* * * * * * * * * * * * * * *   * * * * * * * * * * * * * * * *

Dmin	9 5 1 (E A D)	**EQ**	same		Dm	11 ♭7 ♭3 (G C F)	**GQ**	descend
G7	6 9 5 (E A D)	**EQ**	descend		G7	6 9 5 (E A D)	**EQ**	descend
Cmaj	9 5 1 (D G C)	**DQ**			Cmaj	9 5 1 (D G C)	**DQ**	

Dmin	9 5 1 (E A D)	**EQ**	same		Dm	11 ♭7 ♭3 (G C F)	**GQ**	descend
G7	6 9 5 (E A D)	**EQ**	same		G7	6 9 5 (E A D)	**EQ**	same
Cmaj	3 6 9 (E A D)	**EQ**			Cmaj	3 6 9 (E A D)	**EQ**	

Dmin	9 5 1 (E A D)	**EQ**	same		Dm	11 ♭7 ♭3 (G C F)	**GQ**	descend
G7	6 9 5 (E A D)	**EQ**	ascend		G7	6 9 5 (E A D)	**EQ**	ascend
Cmaj	6 9 5 (A D G)	**AQ**			Cmaj	6 9 5 (A D G)	**AQ**	

Dmin	9 5 1 (E A D)	**EQ**	same		Dm	11 ♭7 ♭3 (G C F)	**GQ**	descend
G7	6 9 5 (E A D)	**EQ**	descend		G7	6 9 5 (E A D)	**EQ**	descend
Cmaj	7 3 6 (B E A)	**BQ**			Cmaj	7 3 6 (B E A)	**BQ**	

* * * * * * * * * * * * * * *   * * * * * * * * * * * * * * * *

```
Dm     5 8 11 (A D G)   AQ   same
G7     9 5 1  (A D G)   AQ   ascend
Cmaj   9 5 1  (D G C)   DQ

Dm     5 8 11 (A D G)   AQ   same
G7     9 5 1  (A D G)   AQ   descend
Cmaj   3 6 9  (E A D)   EQ

Dm     5 8 11 (A D G)   AQ   same
G7     9 5 1  (A D G)   AQ   same
Cmaj   6 9 5  (A D G)   AQ

Dm     5 8 11 (A D G)   AQ   same
G7     9 5 1  (A D G)   AQ   ascend
Cmaj   7 3 6  (B E A)   BQ

* * * * * * * * * * * * * * * * * *

Dm     5 8 11 (A D G)   AQ   ascend
G7     3 6 9  (B E A)   BQ   ascend
Cmaj   9 5 1  (D G C)   DQ

Dm     5 8 11 (A D G)   AQ   ascend
G7     3 6 9  (B E A)   BQ   ascend
Cmaj   3 6 9  (E A D)   EQ

Dm     5 8 11 (A D G)   AQ   ascend
G7     3 6 9  (B E A)   BQ   descend
Cmaj   6 9 5  (A D G)   AQ

Dm     5 8 11 (A D G)   AQ   ascend
G7     3 6 9  (B E A)   BQ   same
Cmaj   7 3 6  (B E A)   BQ

* * * * * * * * * * * * * * * * * *

Dm     5 8 11 (A D G)   AQ   descend
G7     6 9 5  (E A D)   EQ   descend
Cmaj   9 5 1  (D G C)   DQ

Dm     5 8 11 (A D G)   AQ   descend
G7     6 9 5  (E A D)   EQ   same
Cmaj   3 6 9  (E A D)   EQ

Dm     5 8 11 (A D G)   AQ   descend
G7     6 9 5  (E A D)   EQ   ascend
Cmaj   6 9 5  (A D G)   AQ

Dm     5 8 11 (A D G)   AQ   descend
G7     6 9 5  (E A D)   EQ   descend
Cmaj   7 3 6  (B E A)   BQ

* * * * * * * * * * * * * * * * * *


Dm     6 9 5  (B E A)   BQ   descend
G7     9 5 1  (A D G)   AQ   ascend
Cmaj   9 5 1  (D G C)   DQ

Dm     6 9 5  (B E A)   BQ   descend
G7     9 5 1  (A D G)   AQ   descend
Cmaj   3 6 9  (E A D)   EQ
Dm     6 9 5  (B E A)   BQ   descend
G7     9 5 1  (A D G)   AQ   same
Cmaj   6 9 5  (A D G)   AQ

Dm     6 9 5  (B E A)   BQ   descend
G7     9 5 1  (A E G)   AQ   ascend
Cmaj   7 3 6  (B E A)   BQ

* * * * * * * * * * * * * * * * * *

Dm     6 9 5  (B E A)   BQ   same
G7     3 6 9  (B E A)   BQ   ascend
Cmaj   9 5 1  (D G C)   DQ

Dm     6 9 5  (B E A)   BQ   same
G7     3 6 9  (B E A)   BQ   ascend
Cmaj   3 6 9  (E A D)   EQ

Dm     6 9 5  (B E A)   BQ   same
G7     3 6 9  (B E A)   BQ   descend
Cmaj   6 9 5  (A D G)   AQ

Dm     6 9 5  (B E A)   BQ   same
G7     3 6 9  (B E A)   BQ   same
Cmaj   7 3 6  (B E A)   BQ

* * * * * * * * * * * * * * * * * *

Dm     6 9 5  (B E A)   BQ   ascend
G7     6 9 5  (E A D)   EQ   descend
Cmaj   9 5 1  (D G C)   DQ

Dm     6 9 5  (B E A)   BQ   ascend
G7     6 9 5  (E A D)   EQ   same
Cmaj   3 6 9  (E A D)   EQ

Dm     6 9 5  (B E A)   BQ   ascend
G7     6 9 5  (E A D)   EQ   ascend
Cmaj   6 9 5  (A D G)   AQ

Dm     6 9 5  (B E A)   BQ   ascend
G7     6 9 5  (E A D)   EQ   descend
Cmaj   7 3 6  (B E A)   BQ

* * * * * * * * * * * * * * * * * *
```

3-note Quartal Permutations over ii-V7-I Progressions including Diatonic Quartals

Minor quality voicings:		Dominant 7 quality voicings:	
1 11 ♭7	(m11)	9 5 1	(9th)
9 5 1	(m9)	3 6 9	(13th)
♭3 6 9	**(m13)**	6 9 5	(13th)
11 ♭7 ♭3	(m11)	**♭7 3 6**	**(13th)**
5 8 11	(m11)		
6 9 5	(m13)		
♭7 ♭3 6	**(m13)**		

Dmin	♭3 6 9 (F B E)	**FtQ**	same
G7	♭7 3 6 (F B E)	**FtQ**	descend
Cmaj	3 6 9 (E A D)	**EQ**	
Dmin	9 5 1 (E A D)	**EQ**	ascend
G7	♭7 3 6 (F B E)	**FtQ**	descend
Cmaj	3 6 9 (E A D)	**EQ**	
Dmin	1 11 ♭7 (D G C)	**DQ**	ascend
G7	♭7 3 6 (F B E)	**FtQ**	descend
Cmaj	3 6 9 (E A D)	**EQ**	
Dmin	♭7 ♭3 6 (C F B)	**CQt**	ascend
G7	♭7 3 6 (F B E)	**FtQ**	descend
Cmaj	3 6 9 (E A D)	**EQ**	
Dmin	6 9 5 (B E A)	**BQ**	descend
G7	♭7 3 6 (F B E)	**FtQ**	descend
Cmaj	3 6 9 (E A D)	**EQ**	
Dmin	5 1 11 (A D G)	**AQ**	descend
G7	♭7 3 6 (F B E)	**FtQ**	descend
Cmaj	3 6 9 (E A D)	**EQ**	
Dmin	11 ♭7 ♭3 (G C F)	**GQ**	descend
G7	♭7 3 6 (F B E)	**FtQ**	descend
Cmaj	3 6 9 (E A D)	**EQ**	

4-note Quartal Permutations over ii-V7-I Progressions (using the Ionian set)

Dmin	♭7 ♭3 6 9	(C F B E)	CQtQ		Dmin	1 11 ♭7 ♭3	(D G C F)	DQ3
G7	6 9 5 1	(E A D G)	EQ3		G7	6 9 5 1	(E A D G)	EQ3
Cmaj	7 3 6 9	(B E A D)	BQ3		Cmaj	7 3 6 9	(B E A D)	BQ3
Dmin	♭7 ♭3 6 9	(C F B E)	CQtQ		Dmin	1 11 ♭7 ♭3	(D G C F)	DQ3
G7	6 9 5 1	(E A D G)	EQ3		G7	6 9 5 1	(E A D G)	EQ3
Cmaj	6 9 5 1	(A D G C)	AQ3		Cmaj	6 9 5 1	(A D G C)	AQ3
Dmin	♭7 ♭3 6 9	(C F B E)	CQtQ		Dmin	1 11 ♭7 ♭3	(D G C F)	DQ3
G7	6 9 5 1	(E A D G)	EQ3		G7	6 9 5 1	(E A D G)	EQ3
Cmaj	3 6 9 5	(E A D G)	EQ3		Cmaj	3 6 9 5	(E A D G)	EQ3
Dmin	♭7 ♭3 6 9	(C F B E)	CQtQ		Dmin	1 11 ♭7 ♭3	(D G C F)	DQ3
G7	♭7 3 6 9	(F B E A)	FtQ2		G7	♭7 3 6 9	(F B E A)	FtQ2
Cmaj	7 3 6 9	(B E A D)	BQ3		Cmaj	7 3 6 9	(B E A D)	BQ3
Dmin	♭7 ♭3 6 9	(C F B E)	CQtQ		Dmin	1 11 ♭7 ♭3	(D G C F)	DQ3
G7	♭7 3 6 9	(F B E A)	FtQ2		G7	♭7 3 6 9	(F B E A)	FtQ2
Cmaj	6 9 5 1	(A D G C)	AQ3		Cmaj	6 9 5 1	(A D G C)	AQ3
Dmin	♭7 ♭3 6 9	(C F B E)	CQtQ		Dmin	1 11 ♭7 ♭3	(D G C F)	DQ3
G7	♭7 3 6 9	(F B E A)	FtQ2		G7	♭7 3 6 9	(F B E A)	FtQ2
Cmaj	3 6 9 5	(E A D G)	EQ3		Cmaj	3 6 9 5	(E A D G)	EQ3
Dmin	♭7 ♭3 6 9	(C F B E)	CQtQ		Dmin	1 11 ♭7 ♭3	(D G C F)	DQ3
G7	3 6 9 5	(B E A D)	BQ3		G7	3 6 9 5	(B E A D)	BQ3
Cmaj	7 3 6 9	(B E A D)	BQ3		Cmaj	7 3 6 9	(B E A D)	BQ3
Dmin	♭7 ♭3 6 9	(C F B E)	CQtQ		Dmin	1 11 ♭7 ♭3	(D G C F)	DQ3
G7	3 6 9 5	(B E A D)	BQ3		G7	3 6 9 5	(B E A D)	BQ3
Cmaj	6 9 5 1	(A D G C)	AQ3		Cmaj	6 9 5 1	(A D G C)	AQ3
Dmin	♭7 ♭3 6 9	(C F B E)	CQtQ		Dmin	1 11 ♭7 ♭3	(D G C F)	DQ3
G7	3 6 9 5	(B E A D)	BQ3		G7	3 6 9 5	(B E A D)	BQ3
Cmaj	3 6 9 5	(E A D G)	EQ3		Cmaj	3 6 9 5	(E A D G)	EQ3

* * * * * * * * * * * * * * * * *   * * * * * * * * * * * * * * * * * *

Dmin	9 5 1 11	(E A D G)	EQ3
G7	6 9 5 1	(E A D G)	EQ3
Cmaj	7 3 6 9	(B E A D)	BQ3
Dmin	9 5 1 11	(E A D G)	EQ3
G7	6 9 5 1	(E A D G)	EQ3
Cmaj	6 9 5 1	(A D G C)	AQ3
Dmin	9 5 1 11	(E A D G)	EQ3
G7	6 9 5 1	(E A D G)	EQ3
Cmaj	3 6 9 5	(E A D G)	EQ3
Dmin	9 5 1 11	(E A D G)	EQ3
G7	♭7 3 6 9	(F B E A)	FtQ2
Cmaj	7 3 6 9	(B E A D)	BQ3
Dmin	9 5 1 11	(E A D G)	EQ3
G7	♭7 3 6 9	(F B E A)	FtQ2
Cmaj	6 9 5 1	(A D G C)	AQ3
Dmin	9 5 1 11	(E A D G)	EQ3
G7	♭7 3 6 9	(F B E A)	FtQ2
Cmaj	3 6 9 5	(E A D G)	EQ3
Dmin	9 5 1 11	(E A D G)	EQ3
G7	3 6 9 5	(B E A D)	BQ3
Cmaj	7 3 6 9	(B E A D)	BQ3
Dmin	9 5 1 11	(E A D G)	EQ3
G7	3 6 9 5	(B E A D)	BQ3
Cmaj	6 9 5 1	(A D G C)	AQ3
Dmin	9 5 1 11	(E A D G)	EQ3
G7	3 6 9 5	(B E A D)	BQ3
Cmaj	3 6 9 5	(E A D G)	EQ3

* * * * * * * * * * * * * * * * * *

Dmin	♭3 6 9 5	(F B E A)	FtQ2
G7	6 9 5 1	(E A D G)	EQ3
Cmaj	7 3 6 9	(B E A D)	BQ3
Dmin	♭3 6 9 5	(F B E A)	FtQ2
G7	6 9 5 1	(E A D G)	EQ3
Cmaj	6 9 5 1	(A D G C)	AQ3
Dmin	♭3 6 9 5	(F B E A)	FtQ2
G7	6 9 5 1	(E A D G)	EQ3
Cmaj	3 6 9 5	(E A D G)	EQ3

Dmin	♭3 6 9 5	(F B E A)	FtQ2
G7	♭7 3 6 9	(F B E A)	FtQ2
Cmaj	7 3 6 9	(B E A D)	BQ3
Dmin	♭3 6 9 5	(F B E A)	FtQ2
G7	♭7 3 6 9	(F B E A)	FtQ2
Cmaj	6 9 5 1	(A D G C)	AQ3
Dmin	♭3 6 9 5	(F B E A)	FtQ2
G7	♭7 3 6 9	(F B E A)	FtQ2
Cmaj	3 6 9 5	(E A D G)	EQ3
Dmin	♭3 6 9 5	(F B E A)	FtQ2
G7	3 6 9 5	(B E A D)	BQ3
Cmaj	7 3 6 9	(B E A D)	BQ3
Dmin	♭3 6 9 5	(F B E A)	FtQ2
G7	3 6 9 5	(B E A D)	BQ3
Cmaj	6 9 5 1	(A D G C)	AQ3
Dmin	♭3 6 9 5	(F B E A)	FtQ2
G7	3 6 9 5	(B E A D)	BQ3
Cmaj	3 6 9 5	(E A D G)	EQ3

* * * * * * * * * * * * * * * * * *

Dmin	11 ♭7 ♭3 6	(G C F B)	GQ2t
G7	6 9 5 1	(E A D G)	EQ3
Cmaj	7 3 6 9	(B E A D)	BQ3
Dmin	11 ♭7 ♭3 6	(G C F B)	GQ2t
G7	6 9 5 1	(E A D G)	EQ3
Cmaj	6 9 5 1	(A D G C)	AQ3
Dmin	11 ♭7 ♭3 6	(G C F B)	GQ2t
G7	6 9 5 1	(E A D G)	EQ3
Cmaj	3 6 9 5	(E A D G)	EQ3
Dmin	11 ♭7 ♭3 6	(G C F B)	GQ2t
G7	♭7 3 6 9	(F B E A)	FtQ2
Cmaj	7 3 6 9	(B E A D)	BQ3
Dmin	11 ♭7 ♭3 6	(G C F B)	GQ2t
G7	♭7 3 6 9	(F B E A)	FtQ2
Cmaj	6 9 5 1	(A D G C)	AQ3
Dmin	11 ♭7 ♭3 6	(G C F B)	GQ2t
G7	♭7 3 6 9	(F B E A)	FtQ2
Cmaj	3 6 9 5	(E A D G)	EQ3

```
Dmin    11♭7♭3 6   (G C F B)   GQ2t
G7      3 6 9 5     (B E A D)   BQ3
Cmaj    7 3 6 9     (B E A D)   BQ3


Dmin    11♭7♭3 6   (G C F B)   GQ2t
G7      3 6 9 5     (B E A D)   BQ3
Cmaj    6 9 5 1     (A D G C)   AQ3


Dmin    11♭7♭3 6   (G C F B)   GQ2t
G7      3 6 9 5     (B E A D)   BQ3
Cmaj    3 6 9 5     (E A D G)   EQ3


* * * * * * * * * * * * * * * * * *


Dmin    5 1 11 ♭7   (A D G C)   AQ3
G7      6 9 5 1     (E A D G)   EQ3
Cmaj    7 3 6 9     (B E A D)   BQ3


Dmin    5 1 11 ♭7   (A D G C)   AQ3
G7      6 9 5 1     (E A D G)   EQ3
Cmaj    6 9 5 1     (A D G C)   AQ3


Dmin    5 1 11 ♭7   (A D G C)   AQ3
G7      6 9 5 1     (E A D G)   EQ3
Cmaj    3 6 9 5     (E A D G)   EQ3


Dmin    5 1 11 ♭7   (A D G C)   AQ3
G7      ♭7 3 6 9    (F B E A)   FtQ2
Cmaj    7 3 6 9     (B E A D)   BQ3


Dmin    5 1 11 ♭7   (A D G C)   AQ3
G7      ♭7 3 6 9    (F B E A)   FtQ2
Cmaj    6 9 5 1     (A D G C)   AQ3


Dmin    5 1 11 ♭7   (A D G C)   AQ3
G7      ♭7 3 6 9    (F B E A)   FtQ2
Cmaj    3 6 9 5     (E A D G)   EQ3


Dmin    5 1 11 ♭7   (A D G C)   AQ3
G7      3 6 9 5     (B E A D)   BQ3
Cmaj    7 3 6 9     (B E A D)   BQ3


Dmin    5 1 11 ♭7   (A D G C)   AQ3
G7      3 6 9 5     (B E A D)   BQ3
Cmaj    6 9 5 1     (A D G C)   AQ3
```

```
Dmin    5 1 11 ♭7   (A D G C)   AQ3
G7      3 6 9 5     (B E A D)   BQ3
Cmaj    3 6 9 5     (E A D G)   EQ3


* * * * * * * * * * * * * * * * * *


Dmin    6 9 5 1     (B E A D)   BQ3
G7      6 9 5 1     (E A D G)   EQ3
Cmaj    7 3 6 9     (B E A D)   BQ3


Dmin    6 9 5 1     (B E A D)   BQ3
G7      6 9 5 1     (E A D G)   EQ3
Cmaj    6 9 5 1     (A D G C)   AQ3


Dmin    6 9 5 1     (B E A D)   BQ3
G7      6 9 5 1     (E A D G)   EQ3
Cmaj    3 6 9 5     (E A D G)   EQ3


Dmin    6 9 5 1     (B E A D)   BQ3
G7      ♭7 3 6 9    (F B E A)   FtQ2
Cmaj    7 3 6 9     (B E A D)   BQ3


Dmin    6 9 5 1     (B E A D)   BQ3
G7      ♭7 3 6 9    (F B E A)   FtQ2
Cmaj    6 9 5 1     (A D G C)   AQ3


Dmin    6 9 5 1     (B E A D)   BQ3
G7      ♭7 3 6 9    (F B E A)   FtQ2
Cmaj    3 6 9 5     (E A D G)   EQ3


Dmin    6 9 5 1     (B E A D)   BQ3
G7      3 6 9 5     (B E A D)   BQ3
Cmaj    7 3 6 9     (B E A D)   BQ3


Dmin    6 9 5 1     (B E A D)   BQ3
G7      3 6 9 5     (B E A D)   BQ3
Cmaj    6 9 5 1     (A D G C)   AQ3


Dmin    6 9 5 1     (B E A D)   BQ3
G7      3 6 9 5     (B E A D)   BQ3
Cmaj    3 6 9 5     (E A D G)   EQ3


* * * * * * * * * * * * * * * * * *
```

Some Melodic Ideas for Quartals

1. Simple arpeggiation can sound terrific (especially when each chord only gets two beats)

2. Play the following rapidly in succession over Cm7

B♭ F C

C G D

E♭ B♭ F

F C G

G D A

B♭ F C

G D A

F C G

E♭ B♭ F

C G D

B♭ F C

Immediately obvious is the fact that all of the above notes fall into C Dorian.

3. Another way to use quartals in a melodic sense is to utilize the "mega-scale" concept.
   What if we had a scale that was all made up of perfect 4ths???
   How about this 5-note set?

E A D G C

If you rearrange those notes, it's the radially symmetrical pentatonic ur-scale!

A C D E G

Here are some comping ideas for quartals (for keyboard):

1. Play different quartals in the right and left hands (using contrary motion when possible).

   This gives a fuller chord texture and provides more harmonic interest.

   Example (in C):

   Dm (ii minor)
   LH: 9 5 1 (E A D) RH: 11 ♭7 ♭3 (G C F)
   = 1 ♭3 5 ♭7 9 11

   G7 (V7 dominant)
   LH: 3 6 9 (B E A) RH: 9 5 1 (A D G)
   = 1 3 5 9 13

   Cmaj7 (Major 7)
   LH: 6 9 5 (A D G) RH: 9 5 1 (D G C)
   = 1 5 6 9

2. Rootless chords in one hand - quartals in the other. Mix and match.

3. Substitute quartals in the left hand instead of rootless chords.

4. If you don't have a bass player, play your standard walking bass in the left hand and the appropriate quartals in the right.

Adjacent Three-Note Structures in the Pentatonics

A C D	C D E	D E G	E G A	G A C
D7(open) D A C	Cmaj(add9) C D E	Em7 E G D	A7(open) A E G	Am7 A C G
Am4 A C D	D9 D C E (shell voicing)	D24 D E G	Em4 E G A	G24 G A C
C69 C A D	E7♯5 E B♯ D (no third)	G6 G D E (no third)	G69 G E A	C6(open) C G A

figure 75

Three-Note Suspended Chords and Quartals in the Pentatonics
(Note that the following quartal chords are all built off the respective I – IV – V degrees of the A minor pentatonic.)

Suspended chords are inversions of quartals, but may be thought of as either sus2 or sus4 chords depending on the current root.

A D G	D G C	E A D
Asus7 A D G	Dsus7 D G C	Esus7 E A D
G2 G A D	C2 C D G	D2 D E A
D4 D G A	G4 G C D	A4 A D E

figure 76

Chords Derived from the Pentatonic Scale Categorized by Roots

A	C	D	E	G
Am4	C69	D7(open)	E7♯5(open)	G6(open)
A7(open)	C(add9)	D9(open)	Em7	G69
Am7	C6	D24	Em4	G24
Asus7	C2	D4	Esus7	G2
A4		Dsus7		G4
Am7(add11)		D2		

figure 77

While many pentatonic pieces use only triads as their chord choices, there are nonetheless a great many 7th chords (and a few 9th chords) that can be used to great effect in a strictly pentatonic harmony context.

Tritone Substitutions

As long as the root motion is preserved,
virtually any quality of chord can be used in the sequence.

Beginning with the common progression
| G Em | Am D |

we can substitute major chords for the minors
| G E | A D |

or dominant chords
| G E7 | A7 D7 |

Diminished chords are often used for the second chord in the progression
| Gmaj7 Edim7 | Am7 D9 |
All of the above not only work, but are extremely common.

* * * * * *

Using the same original progression (**| G Em | Am D |**), it is possible to substitute just one of the chords in the sequence with a tritone root:

(the examples below only use ROOTS, no chord qualities are indicated)
| G E | A A♭ |
| G E | E♭ D |
| G B♭ | A D |

It is also possible to substitute 2 of the chords in the sequence with tritone roots:
| G E | E♭ A♭ |
| G B♭ | E♭ D |
| G B♭ | A A♭ |

It is also possible to substitute *ALL* of the three last chords with tritone roots:
| G B♭ | E♭ A♭ |

Note that the quality of the chord does not alter the root motion tendencies of the circle, tritone substitute or not.

Granted that the pre-tonic chord is most likely to be a dominant, but the chords leading up to the dominant can be pretty much whatever qualities/colors you choose.

When you have a long circular string, the chords can be altered more the further away from the tonal center you are.

Example (tonal center = G):

Bm7♭5 > E+ > A9 > D13 > Gmaj

The most common tendency for long chains of circular progressions with tritone substitutions is to alternate between minor quality chords for the chords whose roots occur within the scale, and dominant quality chords over the chords whose roots have been tritone substituted.

Example:

| Bm7 B♭7 | Am7 A♭7 | Gmaj |

* * * * * * *

Take this common circular progression:

III > VI > II > V > I

Circular root motion supports chords of any quality:

Examples:

III7 > VI7 > II7 > V7 > I (secondary dominant chain)

iiim7 > vim7 > iim7 > V7 > I (diatonic chain)

iiiØ7 > VI7♭9 > ii°7 > V7+ > I (mixed chain)

Circular progressions using tritone substitutes that form a descending chromatic line:

III > ♭III > II > ♭II > I

Examples:

III7 > ♭III7 > II7 > ♭II7 > I (all dominants chain)

iiim7 > ♭III7 > iim7 > ♭II7 > I (typical tritone sub chain)

iii°7 > ♭iiim6 > iiØ7 > ♭II13 > I (mixed chain)

Summary:

As long as the root motion is preserved (either circular or descending chromatic), virtually any quality of chord can be used in the sequence (within the bounds of good taste). The pre-tonic is usually dominant. It's really all about the root motions, the other chord components are just icing on the cake.

Chromatic Cube Tables 1

#	Color	blue	A#	B (violet neutral)	C	C# (red)	D (yellow / axis of symmetry)	Eb	E	F (neutral green)	Gb (green)	G	G# / Ab (blue)
1	WHITE	A		B	C		⇔ D		E	F		G	
2	RED	A		B	C	C#	⇔ D		E	F		G	
3	ORANGE	A		B	C	C# ⇔	⇔ D ⇔	Eb		F		G	
4	YELLOW	A		B	C		⇔ D ⇔	Eb	E	F		G	
5	GREEN	G#		B	C		⇔ D	Eb	E	F	Gb ⇔ G# *(split fifth of C melodic minor)*	G	
6	BLUE	G#		B	C	C#	⇔ D ⇔		E	F		G	Ab
7	VIOLET	Ab ⇔ *(split fifth of D melodic minor)*	A#	B	C	C#	⇔ D ⇔	Eb		F		G	Ab
8	BLACK	G#	A#	B	C	C#	⇔ D ⇔	Eb		F	Gb		Ab

axis of symmetry

Color category labels: blue · violet neutral · red · yellow · neutral green · green · blue

Chromatic Cube Tables 2

	blue	anti-violet	violet	neutral	anti-red	red	anti-orange	yellow	anti-yellow	neutral	green	anti-green	blue
	G#	A	A#	B	C	C#	D	Eb	E	F	Gb	G	Ab
1 WHITE		A		B	C		D		E	F		G	
2 RED		A		B		C#	D		E	F		G	
3 ORANGE		A		B		C#		Eb		F		G	Ab
4 YELLOW		A		B	C		D	Eb		F		G	Ab
5 GREEN	G#	A		B	C		D	Eb		F	Gb ⇔	G	G#
6 BLUE	G#	A		B	C		D		E	F		G	Ab
7 VIOLET	Ab ⇔		A#	B		C#	D ⇑		E	F		G	Ab
8 BLACK	G#		A#	B		C#	⇑	Eb		F	Gb		Ab

Notes:
- Row 5 (GREEN), far right: split fifth of C melodic minor
- Row 7 (VIOLET), far left: split fifth of D melodic minor
- anti-orange column: axis of symmetry

Glossary of Terms

♯2

Augmented 2nd. An interval of three half-steps. Enharmonically equivalent to m3 (qv).

♯4

Augmented 4th. An interval of 6 half-steps. Enharmonically equivalent to ♭5. Aka "tritone" (qv).

♯5

Augmented 5th. An interval of 8 half-steps. Enharmonically equivalent to ♭6.

11th chord

May contain the root, 3rd, 5th, ♭7th, 9th, and 11th. Often the 3rd is omitted and is used to describe the voicing of a 9sus4 chord (R-5-♭7-9-11).

13th chord

May contain the root, 3rd, 5th, ♭7th, 9th, 11th, and 13th. Often the 11th is omitted.

7alt chord

A 7th chord which contains one or more alterations (♭5, ♯5, ♭9, ♯9). Usually up to the discretion of the player.

9th chord

A 7th chord with an added 9th. May contain the root, 3rd, 5th, ♭7th, and 9th.

A

The note which vibrates at 27.5 Hz, 55 Hz, 110 Hz, 220 Hz, 440 Hz, 880 Hz, 1760 Hz, 3520 Hz

accidental

A note outside the current tonality. May be a flat (♭), sharp (♯), or natural (♮).

Aeolian

The radially symmetrical ur-heptatonic scale. Aka "natural minor", "natural scale".

Aeolian ♭5

The Aeolian scale with a ♭5. Aka "Locrian ♮2" and "Aeolian diminished". The sixth mode of the jazz minor scale.

Aeolian diminished

(see Aeolian ♭5)

alpha cadence

The strongest root motion in tonal music. The dominant > tonic resolution. Aka "authentic cadence". "perfect cadence".

alt7 chord

(see "7alt chord")

altered chord

(see "7alt chord")

altered dominant scale

(see "jazz altered scale")

altered scales

1. Scales that can be used over 7alt chords.
2. Scales which have been altered by a substitution of one or more notes.

approach tones

Melody notes which are used to approach chord tones. May be chromatic or diatonic.

ascending melodic minor

(see "jazz minor scale")

augmented chord

A triad built by stacking M3s. Also any chord which contains an augmented triad as its lower components (ex: 7♯5, 9♯5).

augmented diminished scale

The radially symmetrical octatonic scale which is the ♭5 mode of the "Dorian blues scale" (qv). Aka "diminished augmented scale".

augmented scale

Commonly described as two augmented triads a half-step apart (B C, D♯ E, G G♯), but in this book it refers the "wholetone scale" (qv) instead.

augmented scale (wholetone)

(see "wholetone scale")

authentic cadence

(see "alpha cadence")

avoid chord

In modal harmony, a chord which is not used in a progression because it tends to lead away from current tonic.

B

The note a M2 above "A" (qv).

♭2

Minor 2nd (qv "m2 interval"). An interval of 1 half-step. The smallest interval in occidental musics.

♭4

Diminished 4th. An interval of 4 half-steps. Enharmonically equivalent to M3.

♭5

Diminished 5th. An interval of 6 half-steps. Enharmonically equivalent to ♯4. Aka "tritone" (qv).

♭6

Minor 6th. An interval of 8 half-steps. Enharmonically equivalent to ♯5.

♭7

Minor 7th. An interval of 10 half-steps.

bebop major scale

The flat seventh mode of the radially symmetrical "Dorian blues scale" (qv).

beta cadence

The second strongest root motion in tonal music. The sub-dominant > tonic resolution. Aka "plagal cadence."

black

Relative to the C major scale, it contains all possible alterations except the essential tritone components B and F, as such it is the major scale with its root a tritone away (F♯/G♭ major scale).

blue

Relative to the Dorian, the ♯4/♭5 which is added to create the radially symmetrical octatonic "Dorian blues scale" (qv).

C

The note a m3 (three half-steps) above "A" (qv).

cadence

The resolution to a tonic.

cadential chord

In tonal musics these are also known as "pre-tonic" chords. Examples include a dominant or sub-dominant resolving directly to the tonic (V > I or IV > I). In modal musics, "pre-tonic chords" also exist, but less likely to be either dominant or sub-dominant chords, consequently the term "cadential chord."

characteristic note

The note (or notes) that characterize a certain mode or scale. These are always a tritone component.

chord oscillation

A tonic chord and a non-tonic chord moving back and forth between each other.

chord progression

A sequence of chords gravitating towards a final resolution to a tonic.

chord quality

There are only six qualities of chords: major, minor, dominant 7th, half-diminished 7th, diminished 7th, and quartal. In the case of major and minor chords, the quality is determined by the third degree. Dominance is established the inclusion of both a M3 and ♭7. In both half-diminished and diminished chords, each component is a defining note. Quartals are defined as stacked 4ths (rather than stacked 3rds, as in mainstream tertian harmony).

chord succession

A non-functional sequence of chords, which neither oscillates nor progresses towards a tonic.

chromatic cube

The revelation that all the most commonly used musical scales are intimately related and form a six-sided eight-point three-dimensional structure.

chromatic mode

A "diatonic scale" (qv) played over a bass note not in the scale.

chromatic molecule

The basis for the "chromatic cube" (qv).

chromatic scale

In occidental musics, the 12-note radially symmetrical scale that contains all the half-steps (as defined by equal temperament).

chromatic tetrachord

The "tetrachord" (qv) which contains four consecutive half-steps.

circular motion

Root motion by moving up and/or down by perfect fourths and/or perfect fifths.

composite minor

While all four minor scales contain the same five notes on the bottom of the scale (R 2 ♭3 4 5), the composite minors are formed by sometimes using one type of 6th or 7th and sometimes another.

consonance

Notes which sound harmonious together. Those notes having simple ratios to one another.

cubic symmetry

An illustration of how the components of the "chromatic cube" (qv) relate to each other and their radially symmetrical properties.

D

The note a perfect fourth above "A" (qv).

d

In "quartal" (qv) notation, a lower case "d" indicates a "diminished 4th" aka "♭4" (qv).

D2

Also known as a "sus2 chord" (qv). Here, D2 = D E A

D4

Also known as a "sus4 chord" (qv). Here, D4 = D G A

D5

Also known as an "open fifth" (qv. "open chord"). Here, D5 = D A

defining note(s)

A note (or notes) which must be present to unambiguously define a chord or a scale.

diatonic scale

Any member of the "ionian set" (qv) of modes.

diatonic to …

Indigenous to a scale or mode (as opposed to "non-diatonic", ie. notes which are outside the scale or mode).

differentiating tone

A note which differentiates one chord from another (ex: the ♭7 differentiates a dominant 7th chord from a major 7th chord).

diminished 4th interval

(see "♭4")

diminished 7th chord

A tetrad consisting of stacked m3s.

diminished augmented scale

(see "augmented diminished scale")

diminished scales

Octatonic scales consisting of alternating m2s and M2s.

diminished tetrachord

The "tetrachord" (qv) with the formula R-h-W-h.

222

diminished triad

A "triad" (qv) consisting of two stacked m3s.

diminished-wholetone scale

(see "jazz altered scale")

dissonance

Notes which clash with each other. Those notes having complex ratios to one another (ex: m2 and m9 intervals).

dominant chord

In tonal musics, chords built off the fifth degree of the scale.

Dorian

A radially symmetrical mode of the "natural scale". The fourth mode of the Aeolian / The second mode of the Ionian.

Dorian ♭2

(see "jazz Phrygian")

Dorian blues scale

A radially symmetrical octatonic scale - Dorian add ♯4/♭5.

double harmonic scale

A radially symmetrical heptatonic scale whose formula is R-h-♯2-h-W-h-♯2(-h). Also its modes R-W-h-♯2-h-h-♯2(-h) and R-h-♯2-h-h-♯2-h(-W) (see pg 42). Used mostly in middle eastern and gypsy musics.

E

The note a perfect fifth above "A" (qv).

encirclement

(see "surrounding note figure")

enclosure

(see "surrounding note figure")

enharmonic

1. A note which can have two different names depending on context (ex: F♯ = G♭).
2. A chord which contains the same notes as another chord, but with a different root.

essential tones

In the "chromatic cube" (qv), the tritone components which occur in every one of the scales of the cube.

F

The note a "m6 interval" (qv) above "A" (qv).

flat

A note lowered by a half-step (♭).

fundamental

The note played on a pitched instrument (or sung). The lowest harmonic.

G

The note a "m7 interval" (qv) above "A" (qv).

gamma cadence

The resolution from the ♭VII degree of the scale up to the tonic.

green

The green scale is the octatonic diminished scale formed by the combination of the "yellow" (qv) alteration and the splitting of the fourth degree above the central axis of symmetry (which generates the "blue" (qv) component and the green component).

half-diminished 7th chord

A "tetrad" (qv) whose formula is R-m3-m3-M3. Aka "m7♭5" and "Ø7".

harmonic

Whenever a note is played on a pitched instrument or sung, harmonics are generated. Those harmonics are even multiples of the "fundamental" (qv).

harmonic major

A non-symmetrical heptatonic scale which is a subset of the "Dorian blues scale" (qv). Its formula is R-W-W-h-W-h-♯2(-h).

harmonic minor

A non-symmetrical heptatonic scale which is a subset of the "Dorian blues scale" (qv). Its formula is R-W-h-W-W-h-♯2(-h).

harmonic rhythm

The rate at which chords change and tonality is established.

harmonic tetrachord

The "tetrachord" (qv) whose formula is R-h-♯2-h.

harmony

1. Two or more different (non-unison / non-octave) notes sounded together.
2. The study of chord movement and interlocking melody lines.

heptatonic scale

A seven-note scale.

hexatonic scale

A six-note scale.

hexatonic major blues scale

A type 2 radially symmetrical hexatonic scale whose formula is R-♯2-h-♯2-W-h(-W).

Hz

Hertz = Cycles Per Second (cps). The note A440Hz vibrates 440 times per second.

infra-

Prefix indicating an added ♭2 in octatonic scales derived by adding a note into a heptatonic scale.

Ionian

The ♭3rd mode of the radially symmetrical "natural minor" (qv). Aka "the major scale".

Ionian set

The set of the seven modes which have the Ionian as their parent scale (ie. Lydian, Ionian, Mixolydian, Dorian, Aeolian, Phrygian, Locrian).

jazz altered scale

The seventh mode of the "jazz minor scale" (qv). Aka "Superlocrian", "altered dominant scale", diminished-wholetone scale", "dim-WT scale", "altered scale", "Locrian ♭4".

jazz minor scale

Identical to the Ionian except for a lowered third degree. Aka "ascending melodic minor scale", "melodic minor scale", "jazz melodic minor scale", "Ionian ♭3", "Mel".

jazz Mixolydian scale

The fifth mode of the "jazz minor" (qv). Aka "Mixolydian ♭6", "Aeolian ♮3".

jazz Phrygian scale

The second mode of the "jazz minor" (qv). Aka "Phrygian ♮6", "Dorian ♭2".

Locrian

The seventh mode of the Ionian scale.

Locrian ♮2

(see Aeolian ♭5)

Lydian

The fourth mode of the Ionian scale.

Lydian augmented

Third mode of the "jazz minor" (qv). Aka "Lydian ♯5".

Lydian dominant

Fourth mode of the "jazz minor" (qv). Aka "Lydian ♭7".

Lydian tetrachord

The "tetrachord" (qv) whose formula is R-W-W-W.

m2 interval

Minor 2nd interval. An interval of 1 half-step. The smallest interval in occidental musics.

M2 interval

Major 2nd interval. An interval of 2 half-steps.

m3 interval

Minor 3rd interval. An interval of 3 half-steps.

M3 interval

Major 3rd interval. An interval of 4 half-steps.

m6 chord

The "tetrad" (qv) with the formula R-m3-M3-M2.

m6 interval

Minor 6th interval. An interval of 8 half-steps.

m7 chord

The "tetrad" (qv) with the formula R-m3-M3-m3.

m7 interval

Minor 7th interval. An interval of 10 half-steps.

m7♭5 chord

(see "half-diminished 7th")

major 7th chord

The "tetrad" (qv) with the formula R-M3-m3-M3.

major 7th interval

Major 7th interval. An interval of 11 half-steps.

major bebop scale

The flat seventh mode of the "Dorian blues scale" (qv).

major pentatonic scale

The pentatonic scale with the formula R-W-W-m3-W(-m3).

major scale

(see "Ionian")

major sixth chord

The "tetrad" (qv) with the formula R-M3-m3-M2.

major sixth interval

Major 6th interval. An interval of 9 half-steps.

major tetrachord

The "tetrachord" (qv) whose formula is R-W-W-h.

major third

(see "M3 interval")

melodic minor

(see "jazz minor")

melody

Typically one single note followed by one single note, ie. what the human voice sings. Most melodies are scalar related.

minor blues scale

A non-symmetrical hexatonic scale that is identical to the minor pentatonic but with an added ♭5.

minor pentatonic scale

The ur-scale. Its formula is R-m3-W-W-m3(-W).

minor sixth interval

(see "m6 interval")

minor tetrachord

The "tetrachord" (qv) whose formula is R-W-h-W.

minor third

(see "m3 interval")

Mixolydian

The fifth mode of the Ionian scale.

Mixolydian ♭6

(see "jazz Mixolydian")

modal cadence

The chord motion from a modal cadential chord which resolves satisfyingly to the modal tonic.

mode

Another name for "scale". Most typically it is an inversion of another scale which is commonly regarded as a "parent scale" (qv).

natural

This negates the raising of a note by a sharp (♯) or the lowering of a note by a flat (♭). The natural symbol: ♮

natural minor

(see "Aeolian")

natural scale

(see "Aeolian")

non-cadential chord

In harmony, a chord which cannot be used to effect a cadence to a tonic.

non-defining note

A note which is not necessary to include into a chord or scale to unambiguously define it.

non-tonic chord

Any chord which is not the tonic chord.

octahedron

An eight-sided object with six vertices.

octatonic scale

Any scale which has eight notes.

octave

A note that is double the frequency. Ex: A880 is an octave higher than A440.

open chord

A chord lacking a third degree.

open voicing

A chord voicing using components that are not close together.

orange

In the "chromatic cube", the combination of the "red" (qv) and "yellow" (qv) components to generate the "wholetone scale" (qv).

P4

(see "perfect fourth interval")

P5

(see "perfect fifth interval")

parent scale

The commonly accepted scale of which its inversions are called "modes" (qv).

passing tone

A non-chord tone melody note (or notes) used to move from one chord tone to another.

perfect cadence

(see "alpha cadence")

perfect chord

Type of stable chord that can "stand alone" in isolation without regard to either the previous or subsequent chord, ie. without any harmonic or temporal reference.

perfect fifth interval

An interval of 7 half-steps. Along with the perfect fourth, it is the most consonant interval in the harmonic series.

perfect fourth interval

An interval of 5 half-steps. The inversion of the perfect fifth. Along with the perfect fifth, it is the most consonant interval in the harmonic series.

Phrygian

Third mode of the Ionian scale.

Phrygian tetrachord

The "tetrachord" (qv) whose formula is R-h-W-W.

plagal cadence

(see "beta cadence")

pre-cadential chord

In tonal music progressions, this is known as a "pre-dominant chord" (a chord which precedes the dominant). In modal progressions, this is a chord which precedes the cadential chord leading to the tonic.

primary cadential chord

The cadential chord with the strongest tendency to resolve to the tonic.

pseudo-altered

The "chromatic mode" (qv) built off the ♭2nd degree.

pseudo-Locrian

The "chromatic mode" (qv) built off the ♭5th degree.

pseudo-Lydian

The "chromatic mode" (qv) built off the ♭7th degree.

pseudo-Lydian augmented

The "chromatic mode" (qv) built off the ♭3rd degree.

purple

The purple scale is the octatonic diminished scale formed by the combination of the "red" (qv) alteration and the splitting of the fourth degree below the central axis of symmetry (which generates the "blue" (qv) component and the purple component).

Q

Symbol for a harmonic structure built of quartals from the bottom-up.

q

Symbol for a non-functional melodic harmonization structure built of quartals from the top-down.

quartals

Structures built by stacking consecutive 4ths.

radial symmetry

The concept that the most common scales in occidental musics can be generated by stacking perfect fourths (or perfect fifths) radiating outwardly from one central note.

red

Relative to the Dorian, the seventh degree which is raised, thereby generating the jazz minor scale.

root motion

In a chord progression, the movement of the roots of the chords either towards or away from the tonic.

scale

From the Latin *"scala"* (ladder), ie. structures that consist of "steps", usually either m2s or M2s (but in some cases ♯2s). The most common scales have 7 steps (Ionian set, jazz minor set, harmonic minor set), some have 5 steps (minor and major pentatonics) and scales with six and eight steps are common and useful too. The chromatic scale has 12.

secondary cadential chord

A cadential chord that is not as strong as the "primary cadential chord" (qv), but produces a satisfying resolution nonetheless. Ex: In tonal harmony, the primary cadential chord is the dominant built off the fifth degree. The chord built off the fourth degree still produces a cadence, but not quite as strong as the dominant. As such, the IV chord, in tonal musics, is a "secondary cadential chord."

sharp

A note raised by a half-step (♯).

slash chords

A chord symbol convention which indicates the bass note to be played under a chord. The bass note indicated occurs after the slash (/). Ex. Cm7/D indicates a Cm7 chord played over a D bass note.

SNF

(see "surrounding note figure")

step-wise motion

Root motion or melodic motion up or down by either a m2 or M2.

super-

Prefix indicating that a scale includes a ♭4. Examples: Superlocrian (7th mode of the jazz minor), Superphrygian (3rd mode of the harmonic major).

Superlocrian

(see "jazz altered scale")

surrounding note figure

A way to approach a target note by first playing a note above the target note then a note below it, then finally arriving at the target note (or first below, then above). Aka "SNF," "encirclement," "enclosure."

sus chord

(see "suspended chord")

sus2 chord

(see "suspended chord")

sus4 chord

(see "suspended chord")

suspended chord

Suspended chords do not contain thirds and typically come in two varieties: "sus4" and "sus2". Both are inversions of "quartals" (qv) formed by two stacked perfect fourths. Examples: Dsus4 = D G A, Dsus2 = D E A. "Sus4 chords" have a tendency to resolve to the major triad with the same root (ex: Dsus4 resolves to the D major triad).

t

In "quartal" (qv) notation, a lower case "t" indicates a "tritone" (qv). Aka "augmented 4th," "♯4," "diminished 5th," "♭5."

tetrachord

A "half-scale". Tetrachords consist of four consecutive seconds which can be m2s, M2s, ♯2s, X2s (double-sharp seconds) or any combination thereof. The smallest tetrachord is the diminished tetrachord which consists of 4 consecutive m2s. In common practice, the greatest span of a tetrachord is an augmented fourth.

tetrad

A chord which contains four notes.

tetrahedron

A four-sided object with four vertices.

third

(see "m3 interval" and "M3 interval")

third substitute

By virtue of sharing two notes in common, a minor chord can be substituted for its relative major chord, and vice versa. Examples: Am (A C E) can substitute for C (C E G).

tonic

The "home chord". In most functional compositions, the final chord.

triad

A chord that contains three notes.

tritone

An interval of 6 half-steps. Enharmonically equivalent to both "♯4" (qv) and "♭5" (qv).

tritone substitute

In circular progressions, any chord can be substituted by a chord whose root is a tritone away, irregardless of either chord's quality.

turn

Either a melodic motion or root motion which begins on a note, then moves up-back-down-back (or vice versa).

ultra-

Prefix indicating an added ♮7 in octatonic scales derived by adding a note into a heptatonic scale.

unison

Two notes sounded simultaneously which have the same pitch.

ur-

German prefix meaning "proto-," "primordial," "first," "oldest" "original."

violet

(see "purple")

white

In the "chromatic cube" (qv) the "natural scale" (qv).

wholetone scale

The hexatonic scale consisting entirely of M2s.

yellow

Relative to Dorian, the second degree which is lowered, generating a jazz minor mode.

About the authors

Jeff Brent studied music theory at the University of Colorado. He is a contributor to *Jazzology: The Encyclopedia of Jazz Theory for All Musicians* (Rawlins/Bahha) and also *The Jazz Piano Notebook* (Ranney).

He has traveled all over the world as a professional musician and is the originator of GF-representation, The Fourier-Brent Transform, his Piano Tablature, FB Tonal Shorthand, The 7-Box Sets System for Fingering Diatonic Modes on Guitar, and the concept of Radial Symmetry in music.

Jeff currently resides in southern California, gigs regularly with his jazz combo Trio7 and gives private lessons.

Schell Barkley is an accomplished musician and theorist who has authored many books on the subject of guitar pedagogy, music theory and musicianship.

Titles include his innovative *Breaking the Sound Barrier Guitar Series* and *The Scale Book.*

Schell is the originator of the concepts of the Chromatic Cube and the Chromatic Modes.

Acknowledgements

The authors would like to thank all of those that in some way or another helped to make it possible for this book to see the light of day:

Paris Rutherford III, William L. Fowler, Nor Eddine Bahha, Robert Rawlins, Mark Levine, Adam Neely, Randa Lee, Dave Frank, Vic Juris, Tim Richards, Scot Ranney, Jerry Campbell, Stephen James, Sid Thomas, Rick Zelle, Barry Dallman, Alberto Betancourt, Jon Riley, Brian Prunka, Phil Kelly, Randall Carlson, Jerry Engelbach, The Bakers, Sidney G. Liddle, Mr & Mrs Yves Rue Dieu, Yvon Les Halles, Michael P. O'Reilly, Linda and Janice Weech, Cornelia Lauber, John Signer, John Greet, Hannah Harrison, Brigitte Wolf-Juif, Kimberlee Nicole, Denise Culp, Mark D'Amato, Alfredo, Caleb Lim, Walter Piston, Alex Ulanowsky, Steve Rochinski, Mike Critch, George Russell, Robert Appleton, Sandy Williams, Jason Rogers, Bob Budny, Borys Pomianek, Peter Blommers, Mollie Maillard, Dylan Knutson, and Patricia Ann Phillips.

visit **www.modalogy.net**